Little Book of
PYROGRAPHY

Acknowledgments

I wish to extend my deepest thanks to Chris Reggio, Tiffany Hill, Kaitlyn Ocasio, Justin Speers, and David Fisk for their excellent work in creation, development, and refinement of this manuscript. As an author it is a wonderful experience to be working with such a well-skilled team.

© 2018 by Lora S. Irish and Fox Chapel Publishing Company, Inc., 903 Square Street, Mount Joy, PA 17552.

Little Book of Pyrography (ISBN 978-1-56523-969-2) is a gift edition of *Pyrography Basics* (ISBN 978-1-57421-505-2) with previously published material reproduced from *The Art and Craft of Pyrography* (ISBN 978-1-56523-478-9) and *Great Book of Woodburning* (ISBN 978-1-56523-287-7), all published by Fox Chapel Publishing Company, Inc. The patterns contained herein are copyrighted by the author. Readers may make copies of these patterns for personal use. The patterns themselves, however, are not to be duplicated for resale or distribution under any circumstances. Any such copying is a violation of copyright law.

ISBN 978-1-56523-969-2

The Cataloging-in-Publication Data is on file with the Library of Congress.

To learn more about the other great books from Fox Chapel Publishing, or to find a retailer near you, call toll-free 800-457-9112 or visit us at *www.FoxChapelPublishing.com.*

We are always looking for talented authors. To submit an idea, please send a brief inquiry to acquisitions@foxchapelpublishing.com.

Printed in China
First printing

Little Book of
PYROGRAPHY
Techniques, Exercises, Designs, and Patterns

LORA S. IRISH

FOX CHAPEL
PUBLISHING

Table of Contents

What is pyrography?

Pyrography: The art of burning a design or pattern into a natural surface, such as wood, gourds, leather, or cotton rag watercolor paper using heated one-temperature or variable-temperature woodburning tools or a fine flame.

Introduction

Whether you've never tried pyrography before or you've simply used it for small projects and want to refresh yourself on the techniques, this booklet will show you how to create beautiful pieces with only a pyrographic tool. Today's pyrographic equipment can be both inexpensive and readily available, so getting started is easy to do.

Although it is often referred to as woodburning, the art of pyrography can be worked on just about any natural surface, which gives you a wide variety of possibilities on which to explore this craft. Wooden box tops, gourd bluebird houses, watercolor paper that's suitable for framing, and even leather belts are used as working surfaces for burned designs. For this booklet, I worked the finished samples on several different species of wood, such as birch plywood and basswood; however, the techniques and instructions do apply to other materials, such as leather, paper, and gourds.

As you work your way through the booklet, we will explore what materials and tools you will need for your woodburning kit and how to practice creating and controlling woodburned tonal values through the use of textures and layers. The booklet ends with a section of exercises and accompanying projects, giving you the opportunity to apply what you have learned. With the basic instructions in this book and a little practice, you will soon be able to woodburn any project with confidence and expertise.

Pyrography Systems

There are two types of pyrography systems—the one-temperature unit and the variable-temperature system.

One-temperature tools heat to a preset temperature and create tonal value by controlling your texture or burn strokes and by the speed of your burning stroke.

Variable-temperature tools allow you to adjust the temperature of the tips from a very cool setting to extremely hot.

The number of distinct tonal values that can easily be created increases with the variable temperature tool because you control how cool or hot the tip is during the work.

Options. From single- to variable-temperature units, pyrographers can choose from many options. Your skill level, your goals as an artist or craftsman, and your budget are among the factors that will influence your decision.

One-Temperature Tools

Once plugged into an electrical outlet, the tool gradually reaches an even but high temperature, so the textures you make, the strokes that you use, and the speed of the stroke control the tonal value work in your project.

Using a light pressure to the tip against the wood and moving the tool tip quickly through the burn stroke creates very pale tonal values. Medium pressure and slower motion bring darker tones. One-temperature burning tools are inexpensive, readily available at your local craft or hobby store, and excellent for first-time pyrographers to give the craft a try.

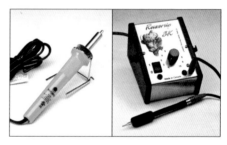

Temperature control. The single-temperature burner on the left takes time to heat up but holds its temperature well. The variable-temperature burner on the right heats up—and cools—quickly.

Pen types. Pens with tips allow you to increase your inventory of tip shapes without spending a lot of money. Fixed-tip pens (blue grip above) eliminate any heat or energy loss where the tip connects with the unit.

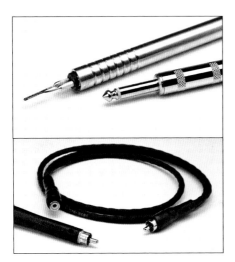

Handpiece wires. Most woodburners use an RCA plug (top photo) to connect the burning pen to the handpiece wire. Some units (bottom photo) use a ¼" (0.5cm)-diameter phone jack for the connection.

Variable-Temperature Burners

Variable-temperature systems have a dial thermostat that allows you to control how cool or hot your tip is. You can adjust the temperature setting quickly, making it easy to control your tonal values in your project. This style has two types of pens—the fixed-tip pen, where the tip is permanently set in the handgrip, and the interchangeable pen, where different wire tips can be used with the handgrip. There are many excellent burning systems available to the hobbyist. Which manufacturer you choose depends on your budget, your pen style preferences, and what is available to you locally or online.

Dual-pen system. With a dual-pen system, plug two pens, each with a different tip, into the unit during any burning session. A selector switch allows the user to change from one pen to the other, and a thermostat controls the temperature setting for whichever tip is in use.

The pens for this unit are slim and lightweight, making it comfortable for long sessions of burning. The handgrip area may be covered with foam wrap or cork to reduce the heat that reaches the hand.

Single-pen unit. Many single-pen units have a range of temperature settings. Changing fixed pens or changing tips on the interchangeable pens is quick and easy. The temperature dial system is very reliable for quick tonal value changes. This particular unit can reach very hot temperatures, and working to the extreme black tones is simply a matter of turning up the heat.

The cork handles are very comfortable and dramatically reduce the heat transfer from the tip to your hand. This style uses a positive, tight connector at the front of the pen for the interchangeable-tip pen, making the exchange of tips easy.

Pen grips. The thick blue foam on the pen above insulates the user's fingers from the heat of the pen. Vents and distance on the pen below move the user's fingers back from the hottest part of the pen.

Adaptability. Most manufacturers sell adapters that allow you to use other manufacturers' pens with their control units. Some units come with a full set of adapters.

Pyrography Tips

Tips come in many shapes and bends, from the tight bend used in the standard writing tip to half circles that can create fish scales and even square tubes that make a textured pattern on your board. Three basic pen tips are used throughout this book—the standard writing tip, the micro writing tip, and a small flat spoon shader.

Standard writing tip pen. For wide line shading and texture work, try the standard writing tip. By holding the pen in an upright position, 90° from the working surface, fine detail lines can be pulled. To create wider lines in your texturing, drop your grip to about 45° from the wood. The angle change allows the side of the wire to touch the board giving you more metal-to-wood contact.

Standard tip sample. The standard tip pen creates a strong, wide line perfect for both outlining and shading.

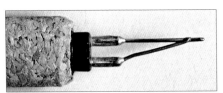

Micro writing tip pen. The micro writing tool is manufactured using thinner wire and a tighter bend at the tip than the standard writing tool. The tip's shape allows little metal to come into direct contact with the working surface and produces fine detailing lines. Fine, dense textures can be layered using this tool to burn an area into an even, smooth tonal value.

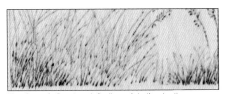

Micro tip sample. For extremely fine line work, try the micro tip pen.

Spoon shader pen. This small flat shader creates a wide path of smooth tonal values and is excellent for general shading within your design. Shader tips come in several profiles, such as spoon-shaped, square, and half rounds.

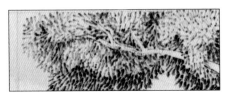

Spoon shader sample. Large areas can quickly be toned using the spoon-shaped shading tip.

General Supplies

You will want to gather a small tool kit of craft supplies for your pyrography. Many of these items are common household items you may already have on hand.

For sanding:

- Sandpaper, from 220- to 320-grit
- Sanding pads
- Foam core fingernail files

Your wood surfaces need a light sanding to create a smooth surface for burning. Use fine-grit sandpaper, 220- to 320-grit, to remove the fine ridges and loose fibers on the wood. Coarse sandpaper, less than 220-grit, can leave sanding lines that can affect the quality of your burn lines. Even fine ridges will cause your tool tip to skip or move as you pull the stroke, resulting in uneven or non-straight lines.

Sanding pads have a foam core and are flexible, making them great for curved surfaces, as on a wood plate or the routed edge of a plaque. Available at your local drug store, foam core fingernail files are a nice addition to your tool kit.

For cleaning tool tips:

- Emery cloth or silicon carbide cloth
- Fine-steel wool
- Leather strop, strop rouge, red oxide or aluminum oxide

It is important to keep your tool tips well cleaned during any burning session to ensure even heat to the tip and consistent color tones to your burning. As you work, notice that the tool tips become dark or dull as carbon from the burning builds up on the wire. The carbon can affect the heat coming from the tip to the wood and leave black carbon smudges on your work. Clean the tips of your tools often.

Scraping the tip with a special tool provided by the manufacturer or with a sharpened knife can quickly clean the tip. Emery cloth, fine-steel wool, or a woodcarving leather strop prepared with either red oxide rouge or aluminum oxide are alternatives.

For tracing:

- Pencils
- Colored-ink pen
- Carbon or graphite paper
- Transparent tape

Two products used to transfer the design to your work surface are carbon and graphite papers.

Both products are laid under your paper pattern so that the transfer side is against your work surface. Both should be used carefully, as they are not easily removed from your work surface after burning is complete. Graphite paper, with its soft pale-gray coloring, is especially appropriate for gourds, papier-mâché, and darker woods.

You can also blacken the back of your pattern paper with a soft pencil, covering it completely. Place the pattern onto your work surface and trace over the pattern lines, leaving a fine line of pencil graphite on your work surface. The pencil lines can later be removed with a white artist eraser.

Smooth surface. Sanding wood surfaces before tracing your pattern onto the medium ensures as smooth a working surface as possible. Paper, cloth, and leather do not require sanding.

Cleaning your tips. There are several methods for cleaning the wire tips of the variable-temperature tool.

And generally...

- White artist eraser
- Transparent tape
- Dusting brush
- Old toothbrush
- Assorted soft paintbrushes
- Ceramic tile or wood palette
- Rulers and straight edge
- T-square or right-angle triangle
- Cardboard
- Canvas stretchers
- Long quilter's straight pins
- Bench knife or utility knife
- X-Acto® knife
- Small round gouge

Many common household items and tools are used for pyrography to prepare the working surface, secure your pattern, trace the design, and finish the completed burning.

If you will be adding paint to your finished burning, you will need an assortment of soft bristle brushes, a paint palette, water pans, and, of course, the thinning media for whichever type of paint you have chosen to use.

Bench knives or X-Acto® knives can be used to carefully carve away small mistakes in the burning and to cut fine highlight lines into an area that has already been burned. Some pyrographers also use them as scrapers to clean the tool tips.

When working on cotton canvas, you will want several sheets of heavy cardboard and long quilter's straight pins to secure the cloth so that you are working on a tight, nonmoving surface. Canvas stretchers can be purchased at your local art store so that you can secure large pieces of canvas fabric.

Also include white artist erasers in your kit. Please avoid pink erasers, as they can leave pink streaks of color on your work surface that are not easily removed. The white eraser cleans up any leftover tracing lines and any oil or dirt from your hands that builds up during a burning session.

Large dusting brushes are excellent for removing the dust created during the preparation stage of sanding your wood surface. Old toothbrushes can also be used; they are also useful in removing any excess rouge from your tool tips during preparation.

BASIC SUPPLY LIST:

- Single-temperature solid-tip tool
- Variable-temperature units
- Standard writing tip pen
- Micro writing tip pen
- Medium or spoon shader tip pen
- Sandpaper
- Sanding pads, 220- to 320-grit
- Foam core fingernail files
- Emery cloth or silicon carbide cloth
- Fine-steel wool
- Leather strop; strop rouge
- Pencils
- Colored-ink pen
- Carbon or graphite paper
- Transparent tape
- White artist eraser
- Dusting brush

- Old toothbrush
- Assorted soft paintbrushes
- Ceramic tile
- Rulers and straight edge
- T-square or right-angle triangle
- Cardboard or chipboard
- Canvas stretchers
- Long quilter's straight pins
- Bench knife or utility knife
- X-Acto® knife
- Small, round gouge
- Acrylic spray sealer
- White glue
- Hot glue gun
- Fabric paint
- Artist colored pencils
- Watercolor pencils

Surfaces

Pyrographers are not constrained to wood. Any medium that is grown or made from natural fibers and is free of toxic chemicals can be burned. A few ideas are as follows: gourds; cotton canvas; rag content artist paper; leather; chipboard; and papier-mâché. We will take a quick look at each in this section.

Because all of our working surfaces are natural products, they will contain small imperfections that can affect the evenness or smoothness of your burn. Wood surfaces have varying grain patterns. For some woods, the grain line will burn to a darker tonal value than the non-grain lines. Papier-mâché—a compressed, glued, shredded-paper product—will have areas that burn more quickly than other areas, creating a mottled effect. Variations in any burning caused by the natural surface are common and simply a part of our art.

The patterns for the projects shown on pages 16–25 are available as a free download online at *https://foxchapelpublishing.com/pyrography.html.*

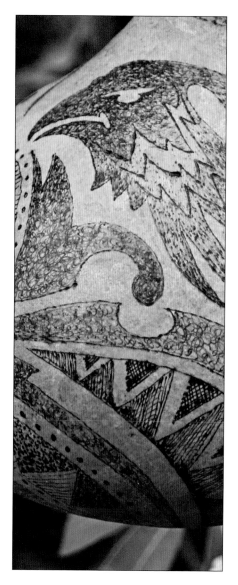

Vegetable-Tanned Leather

Be cautious. Vegetable-tanned leather may have small imperfections that can affect your burning. Be prepared to discover thin areas in the leather, small scratches and dents, and even field brands.

Vegetable-tanned, non-dyed leather is a favorite burning medium for many pyrographers. Available in large pieces, precut kits, and premanufactured forms, including purses, book covers, and wallets, leather offers a world of three-dimensional possibilities.

Leather comes in a variety of weights, from lightweight 1-ounce leather, which is approximately 1/64" (0.5mm) thick, to 7 to 8 ounces, which is 1/8" (3mm) thick, to even heavier belt-weight leathers, which can be 1/4" (6mm) thick. The weight or thickness of the leather that you choose depends on the use and shape of your final project. The sample used for this lesson is worked on 1/4" (6mm) belt-weight leather from a tanned side.

Leather in pre-dyed colors and suede textures is also available, but neither is recommended for burning. The chemicals used to pre-finish and pre-dye leather can create toxic fumes during burning. Suede leather does not provide the smooth, controllable surface for clean, clear burned lines.

Soft surface

Leather has a soft surface, and the pressure of a pencil tracing a pattern on its surface often creates indentations. Use as light a pressure as possible with your tracing ink pen during the transfer process. Once the design has been traced and the pattern paper removed, strengthen your tracing lines by penciling over any light or missing areas. The pencil lines can be erased after the burning is completed.

As you work your leather project, you will discover that the woodburning tip will physically sculpture and shape your design, adding dimension to your tonal work. Run your hand across your burning and feel the ridges of the unburned areas and valleys your burning tool creates. Use this property of leather to give your finished burning a relief carved effect, using the woodburning tips and temperature setting to physically distinguish one area of the pattern from another.

Because of the soft nature of leather, begin burning at low temperatures. Leather burns quickly and tends to go directly to the mid-tone color range.

Using a very low-temperature setting early in your work will help you avoid losing the light, pale tones in your design. For my mapping stage, I work at a setting of 3 as compared to a setting of 5 to 6 to develop the same pale tonal values on birch plywood.

Dark chocolate and black tones are developed using a simple touch-and-lift spot burning. In my experience, leather seldom burns to a true black tone; dark tones often stop in the deep brown range. Please be careful using high-temperature settings—it is possible to burn completely through a piece of leather, especially thinner leather under ⅛" (3mm) thick.

Olson's Dairy Truck. Creating stunning, realistic pyrography scenes requires only a variable-temperature burning unit, a few pen tips, a working surface, and a few common household tools and supplies.

Dried Gourds

Diverse. Gourds provide pyrographers with a delightful selection of shapes that are easily adaptable to craft projects. Turn bushel basket gourds into large storage containers, canteen gourds into birdhouses, and kettle gourds into cachepots for the greenhouse.

With their densely packed wood-like fibers, dried gourds provide pyrographers with interesting shapes to decorate. Easily cut with a craft knife or bench knife, gourds become bowls, sand candle cups, vases, lamps, or delightful birdhouses.

Not all gourds come pre-cleaned, and you may need to remove the skin from the outer surface. As the gourd dries, mold blackens the skin. Wear a dust mask whenever working the preparation steps. Latex or rubber gloves will protect your skin from the dust. Soak the gourd in a warm water bath that has several tablespoons of bleach added. Depending on the thickness of the skin layer, this bath may take up to half an hour. Roll the gourd often so that there is an even layer of water on its outside.

With a plastic kitchen scrubbing sponge, gently work the skin off. I often find that I need to soak then scrub several times to remove the entire layer. When you have the shell area exposed, allow the gourd to dry. You are ready to cut the gourd with a sharp bench knife, a woodcarving tool, or a strong utility knife, and to scrape out the seeds from the inside area.

To create an absolute straight line across the surface of a gourd, as a cutting guideline, fill your sink or bathtub two-thirds full of water. Set the uncut gourd into the basin and submerge the gourd to the depth that you want your line.

When you remove your gourd, you will have a wet line mark across the gourd's surface that is perfectly straight. You can now run a pencil along that wet line as your cutting mark.

Little Book of Pyrography

Chipboard

Extra finishing not required. The completed burning on the *Steampunk Photo Frame* has the look of an old photograph. Chipboard requires no finishing products—sprays or sealers.

Chipboard is an excellent substrate, offering several unique features for the artist. Available in a range of colors from soft beige-orange to solid dark gray, chipboard starts your work in a mid-tone value range much like the old sepia photos common in the late 1800s. Dark tonal burnings become crisp black colorings against the chipboard background. Mid-tone values develop quickly with only a few layers of texture.

Because it is used primarily as a packing material, chipboard is available in extremely large sizes, either through an office supply store or at a packaging company. The thickness of chipboard varies from ⅛" to ¼" (3mm to 6mm).

The cost of purchasing chipboard can be minimal. If you take some time to look around your house, you may have several pieces available for your use. For smaller projects, consider using the back of a stenographer's pad, spiral school notebook, or even the inside of a cereal box. Check any shipping boxes that have arrived, as often a sheet of chipboard is used to line the bottom of packing boxes.

Chipboard can easily be cut using a craft or bench knife and with scrapbook hole punchers.

The thickness of the board prevents cupping or curling during the burning process.

The medium brown-gray coloring is perfect for colored pencil work, making the pale pencil colors such as white, light yellow, and orange stand out boldly against the darker burned areas. Chipboard coated with white paper is also available through scrapbook supply stores, providing the same easy-to-work surface with pure white coloring as your background.

Papier-Mâché

Papier-mâché is a favorite pyrography surface for me. Made from shredded craft paper and glue, the papier-mâché can be pressed into a variety of shapes, from flowerpots to kitchen canisters, gift boxes, and even scrapbook covers. It is inexpensive and requires no preparation steps.

The medium-to-brown-gray coloring is perfect for either colored pencil or pastel chalk application over your burning.

Variety. Papier-mâché is made of the same compressed fibers as chipboard but comes in a large selection of fun preformed shapes. Just about any shape you can imagine is available, from small, comical piggy banks to nesting boxes and holiday decorations.

Artist Paper

Add cotton canvas items such as totes, book bags, and aprons to your list of ideas for your next pyrography project. Fabric burning can create tonal values from very pale soft browns to rich dark russet tones. Any cotton fabric can be used for pyrography, but the thickness of canvas weave makes it the ideal fabric. Also consider working a burned design on pale-colored all-cotton blue jeans, a white all-cotton denim jacket, an all-cotton T-shirt, or an all-cotton canvas tote bag. All-cotton fibers burn evenly and beautifully.

Prewash fabric first to remove any sizing or starch. Blot off excess water with a thick towel so your project is slightly damp. Stretch the damp fabric out over several layers of cardboard, pinning it in place with long quilting pins. When the fabric has dried completely, it will have pulled taut to the cardboard, making it easy to work.

Large paper selection. Art papers come not only in individual sheets but also as rolls, pads, and even premade envelopes and letter-writing papers.

Cotton Fabric and Canvas

Add cotton canvas items such as totes, book bags, and aprons to your list of ideas for your next pyrography project. Fabric burning can create tonal values from very pale soft browns to rich dark russet tones. Any cotton fabric can be used for pyrography, but the thickness of canvas weave makes it the ideal fabric. Also consider working a burned design on pale-colored all-cotton blue jeans, a white all-cotton denim jacket, an all-cotton T-shirt, or an all-cotton canvas tote bag. All-cotton fibers burn evenly and beautifully.

Prewash fabric first to remove any sizing or starch. Blot off excess water with a thick towel so your project is slightly damp. Stretch the damp fabric out over several layers of cardboard, pinning it in place with long quilting pins. When the fabric has dried completely, it will have pulled taut to the cardboard, making it easy to work.

No damage. As a practice board project for cloth, use untreated cotton muslin or canvas to evenly burn a nice range of pale to medium russet tones without damaging the fabric. The designs above were worked on lightweight, unbleached muslin wedding favor bags.

Wood

A large variety of wood species make wonderful backgrounds for woodburning. The most common are basswood, white birch, and white pine. These three woods can easily be purchased from craft and hobby supply stores in precut, pre-routed shapes or as unfinished furniture. Butternut, walnut, and mahogany are also favorites of woodburners; however, they are not commonly found in precut shapes. These woods can be obtained through woodworking supply stores as lumber stock.

Each species of wood has its own properties when burned, depending on the softness or hardness of the wood, the spacing of the grain, and the saw cut direction of each particular piece. Softer woods, such as basswood and white pine, burn more easily than harder wood species, like white birch. For example, a woodburning on basswood done at the same temperature setting and stroke pressure will be much deeper in color tone than one done on white birch. The width of the burned line will also be thicker on softer woods, compared to the tight lines burned into harder woods.

Features to Consider

A number of features come into play when you are choosing wood for a woodburning project. Following are several elements that you'll want to consider before purchasing a piece of wood.

Hard Wood or Soft Wood?

Each type of wood—soft or hard—has unique advantages for the finished project. If you want a dark-toned, dramatic woodburning, choose a soft wood. Basswood can be burned to a rich black coloring, and white pine reaches a very dark chocolate tone. If, instead, you wish to create a woodburning with a wide range of color tones, use a harder wood as your burning surface. A hard wood such as white birch allows for extremely pale coloring, making it ideal for more complex shading schemes.

Working the same pattern (*Dragonette* on page 117) on two different species of wood shows how the wood affects the burning. The upper burning was done on white birch plywood, a hard wood. The lower burning was done on basswood, a soft wood. Notice how the hard wood shows the pale tones, while the soft wood creates darker, thicker lines.

This goldfish pattern (see page 142) has been burned on a piece of heartwood birch plywood. This particular surface contains several swirls in the grain pattern that imply ripples or currents of water. Although the grain color changes dramatically, the quality of burning stays the same across the surface of this wood.

Fine Grain or Coarse Grain?

The width and darkness of the grain of your wood piece also affect the finish of your woodburning. Finely grained woods, such as basswood and white birch, show very little color change in a burned line. Because their grain is so closely packed and there is little color change between the grain lines, these two woods provide a clean, even surface for your work. White pine, however, is different. The grain lines in this wood are very distinct, both in width and in coloring. As you burn across the grain of white pine, you will see your burned line change in color tone as well as in width. This can easily be adjusted by lightly re-burning the pale areas of the line and matching them to the darker tones of the grain areas.

Plain Grain or End Grain?

Wood boards can be cut from the tree log in several ways. Plain-grain wood is cut from the old growth rings and runs vertical to the growth of the tree rings. End-grain wood is cut horizontal to the tree and so includes the central heart section outward to the bark (see *Western Horse* image to the right; pattern on page 146). Growth rings close to the heart of the tree are darker in appearance and are usually wider than the outer growth rings. Heartwood contains a higher sap content than outer-growth-ring wood. Plain-grain wood, therefore, has a finer and lighter-colored grain pattern, thus creating less distortion in your woodburning.

This piece, *Western Horse*, was worked on an end-grain basswood plaque. Looking from the center of the plaque outward to the edge, you can see the tree heart in the cheek area of the horse, the old growth rings of white wood, the new growth ring of beige-colored wood, and the outer ring of bark.

High Sap Contents or Low Sap Contents?

The amount of sap that any particular wood contains can affect the evenness of your woodburned lines. Heavy-sap-content grain burns darker than light-sap-content areas. Since some woods contain grain areas of both low and high sap content, the burned sections of a pattern can vary dramatically. High sap content will also cause excessive carbon build-up on your tip. Clean your tool more often if you are working with high-sap-content wood. Pine is especially noted as a high-sap-content wood, and you can easily see the darker areas of grain mixed with the low-content, pale grain areas.

Light Wood or Dark Wood?

The natural coloring of the wood species also determines the final effect of your burning project. White woods, such as basswood and birch, will allow a greater color range in tonal value than darker woods, like butternut or mahogany.

Untreated or Pretreated?

I suggest that you avoid burning any wood that has been pretreated with preservatives, such as pressure-treated lumber. These preservatives are toxic and can be released into the air as you work. Painted and stained wood also can release toxic fumes when burned since many paints include lead, cadmium, and other heavy metals in their composition. Aged pieces of wood can carry molds and fungi deep within their fibers. As a general rule, it is best to work with clean, fresh, untreated wood as your woodburning background.

Wood Species

There are many woods that can be woodburned and are readily available to the hobby woodburner. We'll take a look at basswood, birch, pine, and butternut, just a few of the choices. Remember to choose wood based on the aspects and their impact on your project. The color of the wood and its grain pattern can be used to enhance the burned image. For finely detailed and heavily value-toned burnings, use a wood with a pale, even coloring and with little grain pattern, such as birch or basswood. However, for a more dramatic effect, you may wish to work on a wood with a strong grain line pattern or one that has a particular color, such as heartwood birch, butternut, or pine. When you are planning a woodburning project, consider the wood's hardness or softness, its color, and its grain pattern as part of the design work.

Basswood

Basswood, although listed as a hardwood species, is an extremely soft wood that is used in both woodcarving and woodburning. It is readily available through craft and hobby supply stores and is often precut as plaques, boxes, and routed shapes. This species is a favorite of woodburners because its grain lines are minimal. Woodburnings on basswood do tend toward the darker tones due to the softness of the wood fibers. Basswood accepts colored pencil very well but does not do well with oil paints or stains.

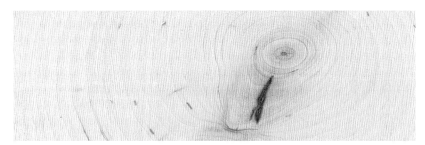

Basswood, End Grain

Basswood also is readily available as end-grain plaques. These plaques are sliced from the log so that the saw cut runs across the tree rings instead of with the grain. Many end-grain plaques include the outer circle of bark, giving the plaque a natural frame (see *Western Horse* image on page 147). End-grain plaques often have imperfections in the wood and in the heartwood, which will show through your final burning. End-grain wood of any species does not color as well as plain grain, either with colored pencils or with paints.

Birch

White birch plywood works wonderfully for woodburning projects. It is a harder wood than basswood, creating a wider range of possible burned color tones. The grain lines in birch are more noticeable than in basswood, yet are pale enough to cause very little distortion to the final burning. Plywood created from birch is available in a wide variety of thicknesses, from 1⁄16" (1.6mm) veneer to the 5⁄8" (15.9mm)–thick plywood used in furniture construction. Colored pencils or oil paints are usually used on birch as a coloring agent. This wood tends to be too hard to accept watercolor work.

Birch, Heartwood Grain

This sample of birch plywood was cut from an area near the heart of the tree. Heartwood in any wood species is darker in coloring and has tighter grain lines than saw cuts made along the outer growth areas of the tree. These tighter, darker bands of grain can create interesting backgrounds for your woodburnings.

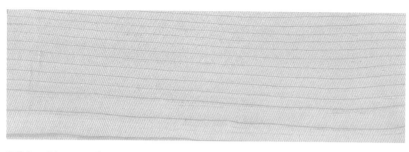

White Pine and Sugar Pine

Like basswood, white pine is a common wood used in craft projects and precut shapes. Unfinished wood furniture is often manufactured in clear white pine, providing the woodburner with larger project surfaces. White pine has a distinct grain with deep lines running throughout the wood. As white pine ages, it will transform into a deep gold coloring or patina, which can affect the coloring of your woodburning. Sugar pine is not as common as white pine. This species has the same woodworking properties of white pine but has a less distinct and tighter grain. White pine and sugar pine will accept colored pencils, watercolors, and oil paints as coloring agents for your woodburning. However, over time, the dark wood grain lines will reappear through the color work.

White Pine, Sapwood

Like the sample of birch heartwood, this white pine sapwood sample was cut close to the center of the tree's heart. This gives the wood wide bands of grain. White pine sapwood also tends to have more imperfections than clear white pine for which you will need to adjust your burning as you work.

Butternut

Butternut is most commonly used in woodcarving but does make a beautiful background for your woodburning projects. This wood can be found in precut shapes through woodcarving supply stores. Butternut has a distinctive grain, like white pine, with deep brown lines running through the medium beige color of the wood. When varnished or polyurethane has been applied, butternut takes on a silvery-gray glow.

Adding color to your woodburned projects is an easy way to give the piece more life. See pages 136–138 for instructions on how to layer watercolors.

Practice Board

That old adage about practice makes perfect is true. Before you start any woodburning project, you'll want to practice on a piece of scrap wood. In this section, we'll discuss the basic techniques of woodburning, like how to create light and dark tones and how to create texture. Then, I'll show you how to create a practice board and give you some exercises so you can hone your skills before you start your project. When you are comfortable with the techniques, we will delve into the theory behind woodburning to discuss tonal values and other ideas that will help you perfect your art.

Using Shading and Texture

The comment I hear the most from people viewing a woodburning is, "Look at all that shading." The shading they are referring to comes from a variety of techniques. In this section, let's take a look at the basic woodburning techniques and how they are applied to create shading.

Creating Light and Dark Tones

As you work any woodburning pattern, you will want to create light, medium, and dark areas within the design. These different tones, or tonal values, are what give depth to the finished image. Several ingredients go into creating the differences between the dark areas and the light areas of a woodburning: temperature of the tool tip, length of time in making the stroke, layering of the strokes, type of tool you use, and type of stroke you use. With practice, these techniques can easily be learned by the beginning woodburner and used to create wonderfully detailed tonal value burnings. All of the exercises in this section can be done with either a variable-temperature tool or a one-temperature tool.

PRACTICE BOARD FOR
TWO DIFFERENT TOOLS

Here is a practice board for creating the tonal values discussed throughout this section. The two left columns were burned using a one-temperature tool. The universal tip was used for rows one through three and row five. The right two columns were burned using a variable-temperature tool. Rows one through three and row five were created using the writing tip.

Row 1: Temperature of the tip. These tonal value changes were created by controlling the temperature of the tool tip.

Row 2: Burning time. Pale tones can be burned by moving the tool tip quickly across the wood surface. Slow movement darkens the tonal coloring of the burn.

Row 3: Layers of strokes. The more layers of burned lines or strokes that you apply to an area, the darker in tonal value that area will become.

Row 4: Type of tip. Fine point tools burn darker lines than wide, flat tool tips. The fine-point tip (left) and the ballpoint tip (right) were used for the one-temperature tool side of this chart. The small round tip (left) and the large shader-tip (right) were used for the variable-temperature tool side.

Row 5: Style of stroke. The type of stroke that you choose and the density in which you pack that stroke also can be used to develop tonal values.

One-temperature tool   Variable-temperature tool

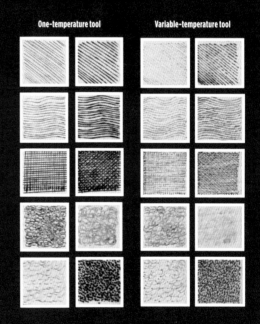

Temperature of the Tip

First, let's look at the temperature of the tool tip. Low temperatures create light-colored burnings. As you increase the temperature setting on your woodburning tool, the lines gradually become darker (see the first row on page 37). As a general rule, begin your burnings on the lowest setting possible. This allows you time to discover the particular properties of the wood on which you are working. Remember that each piece of wood will burn at a different rate, different color, and different depth. A low temperature in the early stages of your project will also allow you to slowly develop and establish the basic light and dark areas of the design. You can then deepen the different areas to create sharp contrast in the work.

Figure A: Hold the one-temperature tool like a pen or pencil. I am using my second hand as a rest and support for my working hand. This provides me with the added height to keep the tool tip on its sharp working edge. The wide heat shield below the rubber handgrip area keeps your fingertips away from the hot burning tip. To burn fine lines as I am doing here, hold the tool in a comfortable upright position.

Practice: Let's take a few moments to try out this technique. Find a piece of extra wood, preferably the same wood that you will use for your first burnings. By using the same wood for practice as you would for an actual piece, you can see how the burning looks on that particular wood and how the wood's characteristics will affect the finished project.

First, set up your work area and find the most comfortable way to hold your woodburning pen. If you are using a one-temperature tool, hold it in the handgrip area as if you were holding a pen or pencil (see Figure A). You can use your second hand to support the hand that's holding the pen. For the variable-temperature tool, simply hold the pen in the foam grip area as you would any writing tool (see Figure B).

Figure B: Hold the pen in the foam grip area as you would any writing tool. Because the tips of variable-temperature pens are much shorter than those of one-temperature tools, your hand is closer to the woodburning surface.

Then, turn on your woodburning tool. If you are using a one-temperature tool, begin burning right away to achieve pale values. As the tool heats up, you will have darker values (see Figure C). If you are using a variable-temperature tool, set the heat to a low setting and burn a few lines. Then, move to the next higher setting and burn a few more lines (see Figure D). Continue this process until you have burned with several of the different settings. For more practice with this technique, be sure to see Light and Dark Exercise One: Temperature of the Tip on page 64.

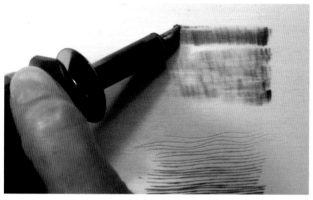

Figure C: Practice burning strokes in different temperatures. I'm using the universal tip on its side and pulling the tool to create broad, burned strokes. The lower lines in this section were done while the tool was heating; the top line was worked at full temperature.

Figure D: Here, I'm using the variable-temperature tool to change temperature. The bottom lines of each set were burned at a low temperature; the top lines were burned at a higher temperature.

Conducting Burn Tests

Once you've practiced with temperature, perform this test to record what your burner is capable of with different types of material. Remember that, for one-temperature tools, your temperature variations come during the time that your tool heats to its top setting. Lines burned soon after you plug in your one-temperature tool will be paler in tonal value than those burned after the tool reaches its full heat setting. Variable-temperature tools can, of course, be adjusted to low, medium, or high heats with the thermostat unit. Set the variable-temperature tool on each marked setting, and burn a line or a small square of a texture pattern into your test board. With a pencil, mark which number setting was used for that line. When you have worked through the range of settings, decide which will be best for your work.

MY EXAMPLE SETTINGS FOR BIRCH PLYWOOD ARE:

Below 4	too cool to use
4	low or cool burns
4½	medium-low burns
5	medium burns
5½	medium-high burns
6	high or hot burns
Above 6	too hot to use

As an example, with my particular variable-temperature tool with a setting range of 1 through 10 and working on birch plywood, I have found that a setting of 4 is my low (or cool) range, 5 is my middle (or medium) range, and 6 is my high (or hot) range. Any settings below 4 are too cool to change the color of the birch during a burning. Those above 6 are far too hot. (Of course, these settings only work for birch plywood. Different settings would be needed if I used a different wood.) Test the temperature ranges available on your burner and note which settings are best for your working style. Remember, your settings will change depending on the material you are burning. It's a good idea to create your own charts based on your tools and materials similar to the one I've created on this page.

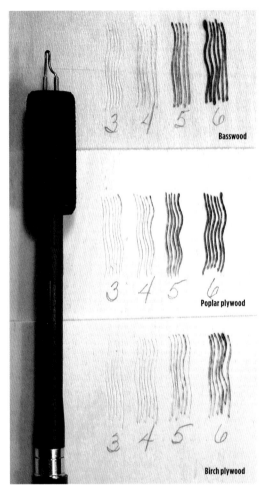

Burning Time

The second method for creating light and dark areas in a woodburning is the length of time during which the tool touches any given area. The longer you allow the tool to touch one specific point on the wood, the darker the tool will burn. Quick strokes create light burnings; slow strokes develop dark burn lines (see row 2 on page 37).

Practice: To practice changing the speed of your tool tip, use the same board that you did for the tool temperature practice. Move the tool tip across the surface slowly to create some dark strokes; move the tool tip quickly for others. You can also try to vary the tool speed in the middle of the stroke to get a gradual change in tone. For more practice with this technique, be sure to see Light and Dark Exercise Two: Burning Time on page 68.

Basswood

Poplar plywood

Birch plywood

This temperature test was done with a variable-temperature tool ranging from a setting of 3 through 6 on a scale with 10 as the highest temperature possible for my burning unit. The top sample board is basswood, the center board is poplar plywood, and the bottom board is birch plywood. You can see that each wood burns differently at the same temperature settings.

The speed at which you move your tool across you work surface determines how darkly it will burn. In the top photo, the upper lines were made by moving the tool across the surface quickly. The bottom lines were burned moving the tool across the surface slowly, making very dark, black-brown lines. The bottom photo shows the same effect with a wire-tip tool—the upper lines were created by moving the tool slowly and the lower lines by moving the tool quickly.

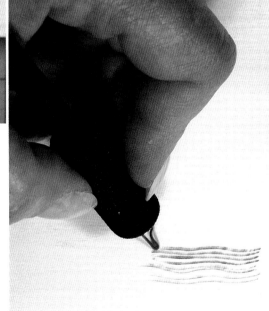

Layers of Strokes

The third way to create light and dark areas is to layer your burned strokes. Generally, the more layers of texture strokes you apply to one area, the darker that area becomes (see row 3 on page 37). Repeated layering of strokes creates dense, thick areas of burning, covering more and more of the original wood background.

Please note here that I have not mentioned pressure. Finely worked woodburning is done by allowing the tool to rest on the wood surface, not by forcing the tool into the wood surface. You should glide your tool across your project using only the pressure that you would normally use when writing with a pencil or pen. Forcing or pushing the tool tip into the wood creates halos around your texture lines so you end up with a deeply burned line, but the surrounding areas also have been scorched to a medium shade. If you find yourself forcing the tool tip, stop your burning and return to a light writing pressure.

It should also be noted here that turning up the temperature on your variable-temperature tool or using your one-temperature tool at full heat will create darker tones of sepia very quickly; however, hot tools can cause bleeding or haloing. A very hot tool tip will burn the area that it touches to a very dark brown or black brown coloring, but it can also scorch the area surrounding the tool tip. This scorching will give a halo of light to medium brown beyond the section that you want burned. By working with a lower heat setting and building your dark tonal values in layers, you avoid bleeding and haloing problems.

In the image to the right, I worked by burning layer upon layer of straight lines. With each new layer, the direction of the line was changed. There are nine distinct shades ranging from very pale to medium-dark. Compare the burnings to the sepia brown value strip and you can see that there are still many shades toward the black that can be worked. This series of brown colors from pale tan through black brown is called a sepia scale, sepia meaning variations of brown.

Because this is the most common method of developing tonal values in a woodburning and because of the wide range of different values you can create, we will look at the steps needed to burn your own tonal value sepia scale. As you work through this exercise, notice that the tonal value is controlled by the number of layers of burning you use within one square. At no time during this exercise is the temperature of the tool increased to create darker colors. Adding layers of burned lines to an area gives you far greater control over the final color depth of that area than turning the temperature of your tool to a higher heat setting.

Practice: First, set your tool at a low-medium temperature. Then, use a soft #2 pencil and a T-square, ruler, or straightedge to create nine 1" (2.5cm) squares on a board of your choice. Leave ¼" (0.5cm) of space between each square. Burn the square with tightly spaced diagonal lines all running in the same direction. In your same square, burn a second set of lines going in the opposite direction.

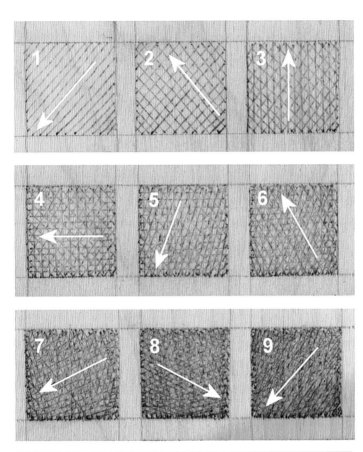

Practice working in layers.
You can see nine gradients of chocolate-toned woodburning. These different shades of chocolate were created by adding layer upon layer of woodburning until the exact color tone was achieved.

Your sample should now look like the second square.

Next, burn a third set of lines running vertically in the area. Your burning should now look like the third square. Continue adding lines until you have nine layers of lines. Compare your burning with each of the squares as you burn.

Notice in all of the sample squares that the coloring is very even throughout the square. Because each new layer was laid down in a different direction than the previous work, the burning takes on a very even appearance throughout the worked area. Any small imperfections in one layer of burning are balanced out in the later layers. By using layers of woodburning at a low-medium temperature, you have total control over both the final color shade of any area in your project and the evenness of that color work. For more practice with this technique, see Light and Dark Exercise Three: Layers of Strokes on page 74.

Type of Tip

Your choice of tool tips also determines the burned value of an area. Wide-faced tips do not reach as high a temperature as fine- or narrow-faced tips because the heat is dispersed across a larger surface area on the tip's face. Therefore, a wide-faced tip will often give a lighter burned color than a narrow tip (see row 4 on page 37).

Practice: Experiment with the different types of tips. You can use the same board that you did for the other practice sections. Try touching fine tips to the wood to create darker impressions (see the top image to the right). If you have a tip with a broad, flat surface, practice pulling it across the wood to make a softer, lighter mark (see the bottom image to the right). You'll also want to try using the sides of your tool tips to see the types of marks they make. Continue working to become comfortable with capabilities of the different tips.

The narrow loop of this tip creates very dark scale-shaped marks when touched to the wood surface.

The large shading tip of the one-temperature tool is often leaf- or triangle-shaped. The broad, flat area of the tool burns medium tones in large areas without leaving individual lines.

ONE-TEMPERATURE TOOL TECHNIQUES

We've touched on a number of techniques in the book. Remember to keep these principles in mind as you woodburn. These simple tips will increase your success.

1. **Keep your tool extremely clean.** As you work, take frequent breaks from the woodburning to remove any carbon build-up from the brass tip. Carbon build-up not only causes uneven burning, but also leaves behind a small amount of black deposit in the burned line. Clean, light-toned lines come from clean tips.

2. **Pay special attention to the very pale areas of any project.** Mark these on your pattern to remember where those pale tones will be. When you plug in your tool, either to start a burning session or after cleaning a tip, it will begin heating. This is the time to burn the pale tones. As the tool reaches its hot temperature setting, move on to the darker areas of the work.

3. **Use certain texture strokes to ensure pale tonal values.** Crosshatching is a favorite because it allows an equal amount of original wood coloring in the texture to balance out the burned lines. By adding more layers to the crosshatched texture, you can slowly develop the mid-tone values. Widely spaced curved-line texturing is another excellent burning stroke for the one-temperature tool.

4. **Apply a light pressure as you work.** The tool tip should slide or glide across the surface. Light pressure allows the sharp edge of the tool to do the burning work; heavier pressure pushes the tip deep into the wood, causing both the tip and the tip's sides to burn the wood.

Style of Stroke

The style of stroke pattern that you use in any given area of your picture gives interest to each area of your work. A lightly burned swirl pattern of curls will give a soft, light coloring that is excellent for shading. Because the curls allow large amounts of the original wood coloring to show through the work, these areas will appear light. In contrast, if you just touch the tip of your tool to the wood to burn a small, tightly packed dot pattern, you can achieve extremely dark areas.

Practice: Again, use the same board that you used for the other practice sections. Begin by choosing a fine tip. First practice creating small, tightly packed dots for a dark area (see top image to the right). Then, using the same tip, make curls to achieve an area that's lighter

A fine tip, like this ballpoint tip for the one-temperature tool, can be used to create tightly packed, dark spots for deep-toned areas in your work. With a simple touch-then-lift motion, this tip will quickly fill an area with black-brown toned circles of burning.

The same fine tip can be used to create a pattern of curls for a lighter area of tone. I used a small round tip for the variable-temperature tool to show how this can be done with either type of tool.

in tone (see bottom image on page 49). We'll work more with this technique throughout the next section, Creating a Wood Practice Board, on page 52. For even more practice with this technique, be sure to see Light and Dark Exercise Four: Texture Pattern on page 79.

Creating texture strokes

In addition to light, medium, and dark areas within a design, you'll also want to have different visual textures within a design. The type of stroke, or texture, you choose for burning a particular part of your work will often depend on the appearance you want to create. For example, a blade of grass close to the viewer would need a stroke that is created with a smooth, flowing line, but a tree in the background might have a tight random curl to mimic the look of leaves and the tree's trunk might have a short dash stroke to imply bark. By using a variety of visual texture, or stroke, patterns within one woodburned design, you add visual interest to each area and element of the burning. We'll look at the huge variety of visual textures you can create in more detail when we get to the practice board on page 52.

Physical, or Actual, Texture

As you create your own sample board, you will notice that some burned lines and visual textures will have actual, physical texture. Low-temperature burnings scorch the surface of the wood. These low settings are enough to change the wood coloring without actually burning a trough or groove into the wood fibers. As your woodburning tool tip, whether a one-temperature tool or a variable-temperature tool, begins to reach the medium to medium-high settings, the fibers of the wood do burn, which creates a groove. Very high temperature settings will burn deep troughs or deep craters down into your project's surface. These grooves, troughs, and craters add actual, physical texture to the work. Adding physical texture through the use of medium to high temperature settings adds interest to the final work. Since low-temperature burnings do not create physical texture in the work, however, the tonal value techniques taught in this book do not depend on actual physical texture; they instead focus on visual texture, patterns, strokes, and layering.

VARIABLE-TEMPERATURE TOOL TECHNIQUES

Remember to keep these tips in mind to aid you in using the variable-temperature tool to your best advantage.

1. **Mark your setting numbers in pencil directly on the wood.** After you have practiced with your variable-temperature burner to discover the color tones that can be created with each temperature, use a pencil to mark that setting number on or near the corresponding tonal value on your tracing. The pencil numbers on your project will remind you as you work which temperature setting you wish to use.

2. **Densely packed line textures can be created in light or dark tones.** Because you have more control over the temperature, you also have more control over the darkness or paleness of the color tone. By using a low setting, dense textures can be created so that little of the unburned wood shows, yet the sepia, or brown, tone is extremely pale in value.

3. **Develop your tonal values slowly through layers, not through heat.** Just because you can turn a variable-temperature tool on its highest setting for very dark areas does not mean that quick, hot burnings are always the best for black areas in your design. There are many tones of color possible between dark brown and black. By developing the burning slowly through layers, you can choose which tone works best for each area.

4. **Keep your tips extremely clean.** Develop the habit of cleaning and polishing the tips often and thoroughly to ensure the best quality of line possible.

Creating a Wood Practice Board

One of the fun ways to learn to control your woodburning strokes is to create a practice board. This gives you a working surface on which to experiment with the wide variety of strokes you will use. It can also be used to record any new strokes and layering techniques you discover as you grow in this craft. Plus, because this board is only used as practice, it is a great place to work until you learn to control your strokes. Once you have control over the stroke, you can move to your working project with confidence.

I also use my practice board to work out textures and specific elements of a pattern. Small pattern samples not only let me create the textures I want to use, but they also help me establish the lights and darks in a pattern before I start on my actual project.

My practice boards are usually made on birch plywood because this is the wood species that I use the most. You may wish to make your practice board on your favorite wood surface so your practice work will show you the same burns as those on your finished projects.

The most basic practice board, and the one I recommend all beginning pyrographers create, is laid out as a grid pattern on the wood. I used a soft #2 pencil and a T-square to section my board into 1" (2.5cm) squares with ¼" (0.5cm) spacing between each square. As you begin each new project or approach a texture that you have not done before, try it out first on your practice board. Number each square with a pencil so you may keep a corresponding card file for each square, noting the particular tool tip you used, the temperature settings for the burner, and on which project you used the texture.

Keep your practice board close to your work area. This makes it quick and easy to add new textures, and it will be handy for choosing previously tested textures for a new project.

Creating textures. Mark a 10" x 12" (25.5 x 30.5cm) sheet of poplar or birch plywood or a piece of basswood into five rows of 1" (2.5cm) squares with a pencil. Use the grid squares to create each new texture.

Temperature settings

In the example (page 53), for my first row (right row A) I set the burner temperature setting at 5 and then filled the top square with a random curling doodle stroke. The square below it was worked on setting 6, then setting 7 through to setting 9. With each temperature change, the tonal value became darker. I marked my temperature setting in pencil to the right of each square for easy reference later.

Three Common Fill Patterns

Three common fill patterns used in pyrography are cross-hatching, random doodles, and the scrubbie stroke.

Cross-hatching fills an area with layers of fine parallel lines. Each new layer is laid on a diagonal to the last, slowly developing the depth of the tonal value.

Make the **random doodle stroke** by working tightly packed loops. As the new looping line crosses an older line, the area becomes denser and therefore darker.

The **scrubbie** is a short back-and-forth stroke that quickly fills an area. The space between each of those back-and-forth strokes—how much unburned area is allowed—establishes your tonal depth.

As you work your practice board, you will discover the fill strokes that are the most comfortable or natural for you to use in your style of work.

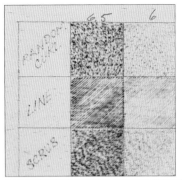

Marking the board. Make pencil notations on your practice board for both the temperature setting and pen tip used.

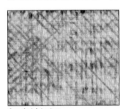

Crosshatch texture

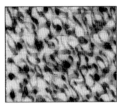

Random doodle

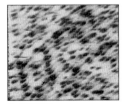

Scrubbie stroke

Quick Reference Texture Chart

By creating a practice board that you keep close to your work area, you can test new textures, tonal values, and even small pieces of a design before you begin work on your project surface. Try creating the practice board pictured on page 57 by following this chart.

Square #	Texture Name	Tonal Value
1–5	Dash Stroke	Pale to dark tones
6–14	Linear Circles	Pale value to dark tones
15–23	Wide-Spaced Crosshatch	Medium to black tones
24–32	Tight-Spaced Crosshatch	Medium to black tones
33–37	Random Curls	Pale to dark tones
38	Check Marks	Medium to dark tones
39	Wide-Spaced Zigzag	Medium tone
40	Random Zigzag	Medium tone
41	Sun Rays or Grass Strokes	Medium tone
42	Wavy Lines	Medium to dark tones
43	Seashell Circles	Dark tones
44	Tightly Packed Zigzag	Medium tone
45	Tight Circles	Medium to dark tones
46	ABC	Dark tone
47	568	Dark tone
48	Scales	Dark tone
49	SUE	Medium to dark tones
50	Mountain Peaks	Dark tone
51	Quilting	Medium tone
52	Overlapping Hearts	Medium tone
53	Herringbone	Medium to dark tones
54	Diagonal Ripples	Medium to dark tones

Square #	Texture Name	Tonal Value
55	Water Ripples	Medium to dark tones
56	Tightly Packed Spots	Dark to black tones
57	Long Scales	Dark to black tones
58	Close-up Branches and Leaves	Medium to black tones
59	Wood Grain	Pale to dark tones
60	Tall Grass Clumps	Medium to dark tones
61–64	Scrubbie Lines	Pale to dark tones
65	Small Crosshatched Elements	Pale to dark tones
66–68	Straight Lines	Pale to dark tones
69	Long Curved Line	Pale to dark tones
70	Short Curved Line	Pale to dark tones
71	Veining Curved Line	Pale to dark tones
72	Background Trees	Medium to dark tones
73	Tall Grass	Pale to dark tones
74	Stone Walkway	Medium tones
75	Evergreens	Pale to dark tones
76	Deciduous Trees	Pale to dark tones
77	Pines and Deciduous Shrubs	Pale to dark tones
78	Roof and Shadows	Pale to dark tones
79	Barn Boards	Pale to dark tones
80	Bricks	Pale to dark tones
81	Small Pine and Shrub	Pale to dark tones

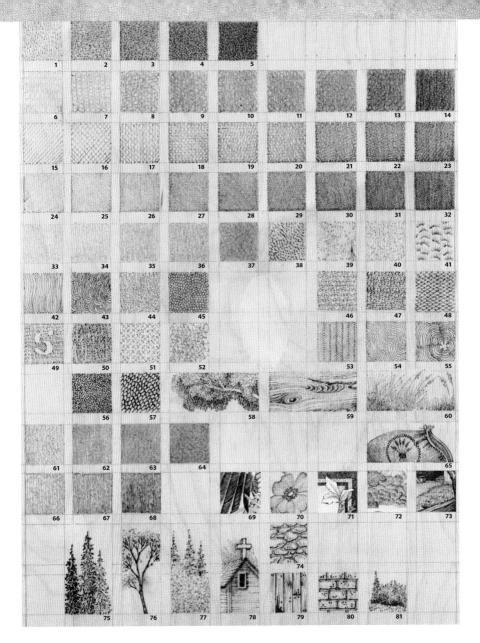

Tonal Values Practice Board

(Uses pattern on page 63.)

Tonal or gray scale values refer to how dark or light a burned area appears in your work. The palest values in a woodburning are those not burned at all. Instead, the raw wood is used for the sepia tone of that area. The darkest tonal value will be areas you burn at high temperatures to a near-black tone. A range of tones, from pale tans to mid-browns and on into dark browns, falls between the two extremes.

This range of tonal values, worked from the palest progressively through the mid-tones into the black, is called a tonal value scale. Tonal value scales are called gray scales when you are working with black-and-white photographs. For woodburnings, they are called sepia value scales because of the soft beige through rich deep browns of the burned wood.

In woodburning, how pale or dark your tonal value for an area becomes depends on the temperature setting of your burning unit, the time the tip touches the wood, and how loosely or tightly packed your burn strokes are in an area.

The tiger portrait is divided into five tonal values:

- **black** for around the eyes, nose, and mouth
- **dark** for the wide facial stripes
- **medium** for the shading along the sides of his face, chin, and nose
- **pale** for light shading through the nose, forehead, and under the eyes
- **white** (unburned) areas in what would be the white stripes of his face.

SUPPLIES:

- 8" x 8" (20 x 20cm) birch plywood
- variable-temperature burning unit
- standard writing tip
- matte acrylic spray sealer

Bengal Tiger. A study in tonal value scales on wood.

1 **Dark tonal value.** After tracing the pattern to the wood, I worked my dark tonal values using a medium-high temperature setting. For my unit, that is a setting between 6 and 6.5 on the dial. I used a tightly packed short line stroke that was worked with the direction of the wood grain. As I worked, I moved the tool tip in a slow, smooth motion across the wood. The slow motion, tightly packed strokes, and medium-high setting gave me an even deep brown tonal value.

Scrubbie stroke. The scrubbie stroke is made with a quick back-and-forth motion. The number of small scrubbie lines, the temperature setting, and the number of layers of burning determine the tonal value.

2 **Medium tonal value.** To lighten the tonal value in the next areas to be burned, I turned down my temperature setting to just below 6, a medium setting for my unit. Otherwise, I used the same slow movement with the grain to burn the tightly packed short line strokes. The simple adjustment to my temperature setting created a new tonal value of medium brown.

Short strokes. Because the scrubbie stroke uses very short lines, there is a large amount of overlapping in any one layer of work. The overlap creates small dark spots and extra dark lines—perfect for a tiger's fur. Working the stroke with the grain of the birch plywood adds to the fur effect.

3 **Pale tonal value.** For my pale-value burned areas, I turned down my temperature setting to about 5.5, a low-medium setting for my unit. I increased the speed of my burning motion, which kept the tool tip on the wood for a minimal amount of time. I also allowed more space between each short line stroke. This small amount of space allows some of the raw wood to show through the burned area, helping to keep this area in a pale-tan tonal value.

4 **Black tonal value.** My black tones were worked last by turning my temperature back to 6.5 and using a very slow motion with the tool tip. Again, I used a tightly packed short line stroke to fill the areas around the eyes, nostrils, and mouth. I now have a completed burning with little or no texture and no outlining or detailing. The entire pattern was worked by using only four burned tonal values and the white of the raw, unburned wood. With tonal values alone I created a Bengal tiger's face. The completed project has distinct tonal values from the white of the wood through the black tones surrounding the eyes.

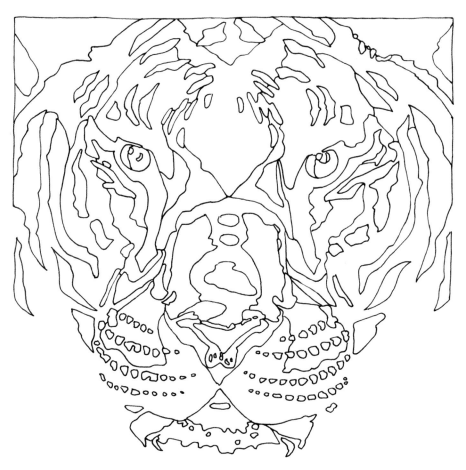

© Lora S. Irish

Bengal Tiger
Enlarge pattern 154%
for actual size.

Exercises for Practice

Now that you know how to create different tonal values and textures and have worked on a practice board, here are some exercises for practicing some of the different techniques. Go ahead and try the whole pattern if you want, or you can just try parts of the pattern to further explore its listed skill. Unless otherwise stated, the practice projects in this section were worked using a variable-temperature tool with the writing tip on birch plywood. If you are working with a one-temperature tool, please use the universal tip. Heat settings are noted for each project.

Light and Dark Exercise One:

Temperature of the Tip

The wheat design used in *Our Daily Bread* (pattern on page 67) is created with a simple straight-line fill texture (see the photos at the right and squares 66–68 on page 57). The coloring of each line in the wheat—whether it is light, medium, or dark—is controlled by the temperature of the tool. Notice in this finished sample that all of the woodburned lines run vertically within the design and that no element of the pattern has been outlined.

Tips for completing the entire pattern:

- Use a medium-high or high setting to burn the sections that are turned back on the bottom cross leaves and the tall pale leaves.

- The lettering is done in very close, tightly packed, short lines to create the darkest burning on the board.

Our Daily Bread. Even though this burning uses only one texture, the straight line, it has three distinct tonal values: dark, medium, and light. How cool or hot you set your variable-temperature tool determines the tonal value of the burned stroke.

1 **Here is a small wheat pattern** that you can use on your practice board to learn to control the tonal values through your temperature settings on your variable-temperature tool.

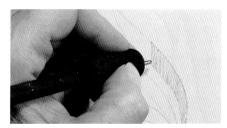

2 **Once the sample pattern has been traced**, set your thermostat to a very low setting. Start your project with the tallest pale leaf. Pull long, light-colored lines from the top of the leaf to the bottom section, touching the traced line at both points. Fill that leaf with closely packed parallel lines using your writing tip.

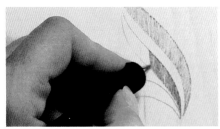

3 **Turn your thermostat up** to a medium temperature setting. Fill the second wheat leaf with parallel lines using the writing tip. Notice that these lines burn slightly darker than the lines in the first leaf.

4 **By turning up your thermostat one more time** to a medium-high or high setting, you can now fill the last, third leaf with dark-toned lines.

5 **The wheat head** has three rows of seeds. The center row is burned using a low setting; the right-side row uses a medium setting; and the left-side row, the stem, and the wheat whiskers are burned at a medium-high or high setting.

6 **Once all of the burning is done,** use a white artist's eraser to remove any remaining pencil graphite from the tracing and very lightly sand the surface with an emery board. Because each area was created using the same texture—the straight-line fill—the pattern's depth of color was established solely through the temperature settings of the tool.

Our Daily Bread
Enlarge pattern 171% for actual size.

© Lora S. Irish

Light and Dark Exercise Two:

Burning Time

For the pattern *Wild Rose Corner* (on page 78), the thermostat for the woodburning tool was set at a medium range throughout the work (see the photos at the right). The changes in the coloring—the darkness of the wide borderline to the lightness of the leaves—were determined by how long the tool remained on the wood during the burning. Slow strokes created the dark areas; faster strokes made light lines.

Tips for completing the entire pattern:

- Begin by working the texture pattern that lies behind the borderlines and flower design. This texture is a simple swirl design, created by moving your tool in very small, random curls across the wood (see squares 33–37 on page 57). Start this curl pattern at the inner corner of the wide borderline; this is your darkest area for the background work. Move the tool slowly throughout this area to burn a medium-toned coloring. As you work away from the corner toward the outside of the pattern area, increase the speed with which you move your tool. Slightly faster burning will create paler curled lines. Continue filling in the background, gradually increasing the speed of your stroke until you can barely see the burn lines along the farthest edges of the work.

- The stems on the rose are done with short straight-line fill strokes (see squares 66–68 on page 57), allowing the tool to touch the wood long enough to create a medium-dark tone. The dark shading in the rose stems is done by repeating the burning over these areas. This gives two layers to the shaded side of the stem.

- The outline on the flower petals is darker at the base of the flower and becomes pale toward the outer edge.

- The veins in the flower petals, rosebud, flower center, and leaves are done in gently curved lines (see squares 69–70 on page 57) at a medium stroke speed.

- Work the petal lines from both the outer edge of the petal toward the center and then from the center of the petal toward the flower center, creating two sets of lines within each petal.

- Work the flower center from the central circle.

- Use tightly packed spots (see square 56 on page 57) to create small dots on the center lines of the rose and in the deep areas of the rosebud.

Wild Rose Corner. A wide range of values can be created just by learning to control how much time you use to make an individual burned stroke.

1 **This three rose leaf pattern** will let you learn how the speed of the tool affects the tonal value of the burned line or area. As with the exercise for *Our Daily Bread*, this small design can be worked on your practice board.

2 **Trace the design** to your practice board. Set the temperature of your variable-temperature tool to a medium heat. Start by outlining the leaves. Move the tool slowly so that the tool tip can burn a dark line along the edge of each leaf. Increase your speed as you approach a stop area. Notice where the leaf notches touch. The line closest to that joint is darker than the line at the tip of the leaf.

3 **Begin the stroke at the center vein** and pull your tool toward the outer edge of the leaf. The veins are done in gently curved lines (see squares 69–70 on page 57) at a medium stroke speed. Notice how the line is darkest where it touches the center vein and then pales as you pull the tool away from that vein. This happens because your tool tip is hottest when it first touches the wood. As the tip is pulled through a stroke, it begins to cool slightly, therefore lightening the end of the burned line. You can use this to your advantage in a design. Starting the stroke, its darkest point, at the center vein area of a leaf, for example, gives emphasis to the center vein.

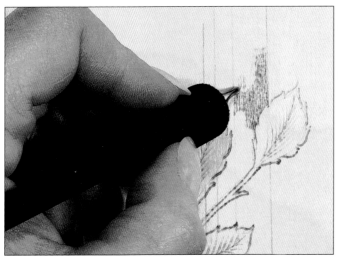

4 **The large wide line** behind the leaves is worked with a scrubbie line texture an even, smooth movement.

5 **Watch the color of the burning** as you begin working this area. If the color seems pale, slow the tip movement to allow more burning time with each stroke. An early dark tone may mean that you need to move the tool more quickly to achieve a medium tonal value.

6 **The thin background line** is filled with a tightly packed spot that is created by touching the tool tip to the board and then lifting. This touch-and-lift action creates small dark dots on your board (see square 56 on page 57).

7 **To develop a small amount of contrast color**, or tone, in the background behind the white, unburned areas of the leaves, a curled line or circular stroke is used with a quick, flowing motion. Faster movements with your tool tips burn very pale shades of brown. I found it easier to turn the board upside down for this step.

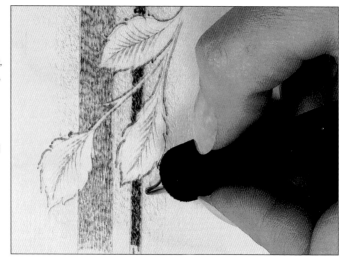

8 **When the burning is complete**, erase any remaining pencil-tracing lines and lightly sand. Although the heat setting was never changed during this exercise, you can create a wide variety of brown tones with just the speed of the movement of your burning tip.

Layers of Strokes

The light and dark areas in the *Ivy Line* design (pattern on page 78) were created by adding layer upon layer of burned strokes to the different areas (see the photos at the right). The number of layers determines the lightness or darkness of each element within the pattern. The simplest stroke for layer work is the tightly spaced crosshatch pattern (see squares 24–32 on page 57). Here, straight lines are laid down with all of the lines in that layer going in one direction. With each new layer the lines are burned in a new direction. I used a medium heat setting for this exercise.

Tips for completing the entire pattern:

- *Ivy Line* has four different shades of light and dark: There is a very pale set of leaves that uses one layer of lines (1); the medium-colored leaves use two layers (2); the darkest leaves use three layers (3); and the borderline is done in a short-line fill texture (4). This design is not outlined.

- The borderlines are burned using tightly packed spots (see square 56 on page 57).

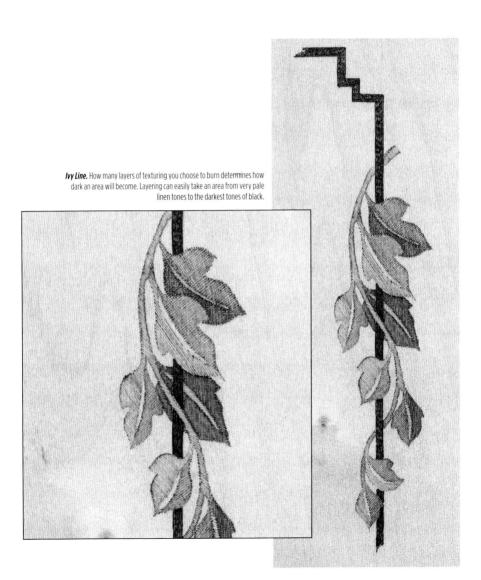

Ivy Line. How many layers of texturing you choose to burn determines how dark an area will become. Layering can easily take an area from very pale linen tones to the darkest tones of black.

1 **A simple ivy leaf pattern** is perfect for learning to use layers of burning to create tonal value changes in a project. Add this small design to your practice board.

2 **Begin burning** tightly packed parallel lines into both sides of the leaf pattern at a 45-degree angle to the design (see square 24 on page 57). Space your lines evenly as you work. Notice in the sample that the width of the unburned wood is about the same size as the width of the burned line. Start each line at the top of the pencil-tracing line and pull it until it touches the bottom tracing line of that section of leaf.

3 **On one side of the leaf**, burn a second layer of tightly packed parallel lines. These lines should run 90 degrees to the lines in your first layer of burning (see square 25 on page 57). Notice that this second layer makes that side of the leaf darker in tone than the other side.

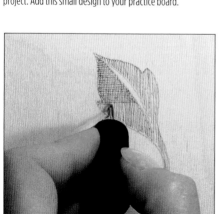

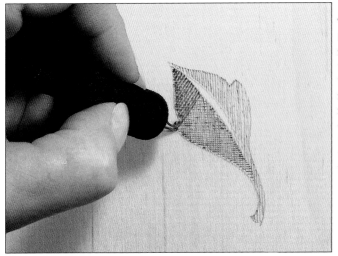

4 A third layer of tightly packed parallel lines

has been burned into the dark side of the leaf. This layer is worked at a 45-degree angle to the previous layer (see square 26 on page 57). You should have two very different colors, or tones, of brown in the two sides of your leaf when you are done with the third layer.

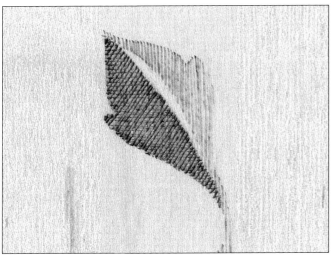

5 When the work is complete, erase your

pencil lines and lightly sand. Changing the number of layers you burn with cross-hatching is a simple and foolproof way to create different tonal values.

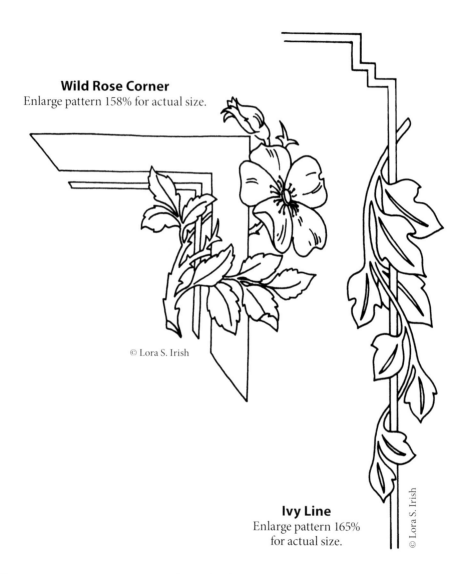

Wild Rose Corner
Enlarge pattern 158% for actual size.

© Lora S. Irish

Ivy Line
Enlarge pattern 165%
for actual size.

© Lora S. Irish

Light and Dark Exercise Four:
Texture Pattern

So far in our practice projects we have used straight lines, cross-hatching, random curls, and the short-line fill stroke, but any pattern of burning can be used to create the dark and light areas in your woodburning design (see the photos at the right). For *My Room Gingerbread Man* (pattern on page 83) I chose to burn the background areas using three capital letters: A, B, and C (see square 46 on page 57). Be creative with the texture pattern that you choose for this project. This pattern could easily be done by using 1, 2, 3 or by using a child's name, such as "AMY" or "JEFFREY." The words "My Room" could also be replaced with your child's name. I used a medium setting for this exercise.

The *My Room Gingerbread Man* pattern is too detailed to practice just a part, so we will practice the negative space technique with the letter A. In order to form a negative element, shading must be especially dark on the borders of the object to emphasize and define its edges. I chose random curls for this exercise, but you can choose any fun texture you want!

Tips for completing the entire pattern:

- Although I have burned my sample on a piece of birch plywood, this particular pattern would be delightful done on a gingerbread man cut-out shape or a door hanger sign.

- Using a T-square, ruler, and soft #4B to #6B pencil, mark guidelines across the wood for your letter placement. Because this pattern is fairly tall, I used a spacing of ⅛" (0.5cm).

- When you reach an area on the inner design—the eyes, mouth, icing trim, or words "My Room"—stop burning. Notice with this pattern that the woodburned areas are used to surround the actual important elements of the design.

My Room Gingerbread Man. Not only has this design been worked with an unusual texturing pattern, it is also done as a negative pattern, or negative image. The woodburning has been worked to surround the main elements (the lettering and face) of the pattern, and therefore make the unburned areas of the gingerbread man stand out.

1 **Add this small pattern** to your practice board.

2 **Working with any of the three techniques** that we are discussing in this section—temperature, burning time, and layers—begin to shade in all of the space surrounding the letter A to a pale or light tone of brown.

3 **As you work, darken the areas** that are nearest the letter A to a medium tone. Notice how the letter begins to stand out from its background even though you have done no woodburning to the letter itself.

4 **Your darkest tonal value** of brown should be where the background directly touches the letter. Don't outline the letter; instead, darken the background.

5 **Erase your guidelines** and pattern lines, and then lightly sand the surface. Dark tonal values can make unburned or unworked areas of your project stand out against their brown backgrounds. Dramatic changes in tonal values create a striking finish for a pattern.

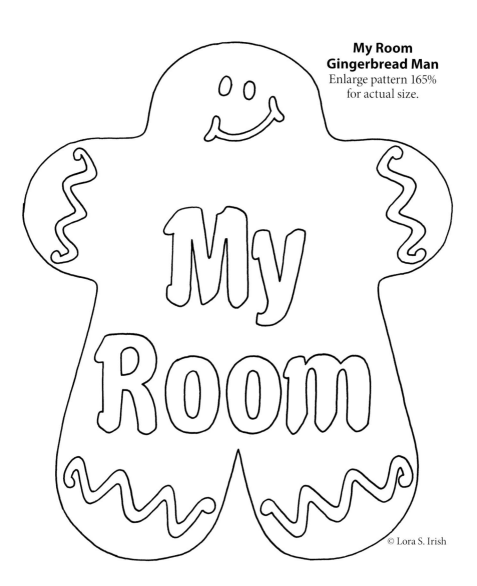

My Room Gingerbread Man
Enlarge pattern 165% for actual size.

© Lora S. Irish

Light and Dark Exercise Five:
Putting It All Together

In *Buffalo Skull Dream Weaver Circle* (pattern on page 88) I have put all of these methods together to create a work that has several points of interest (see the photos at the right). The first thing that you may notice is the dramatic changes in shading. The paleness of the buffalo skull is balanced by the extremely dark surrounding circles of the dream catcher. Second, each area of the woodburning has its own texturing stroke. Because this exercise includes so many different textures and techniques, we will be working with the whole pattern instead of using a portion of the pattern as we did with the previous exercises.

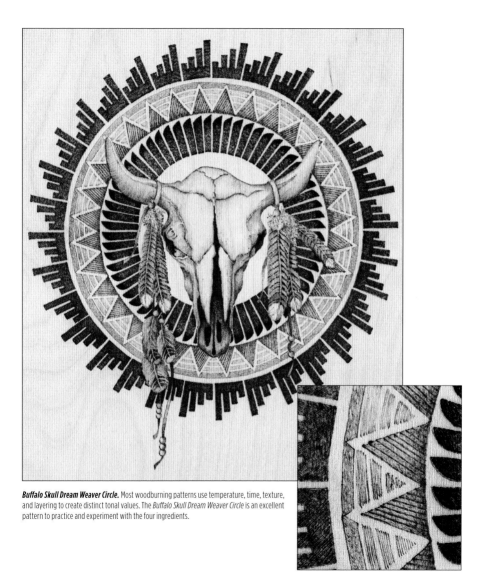

Buffalo Skull Dream Weaver Circle. Most woodburning patterns use temperature, time, texture, and layering to create distinct tonal values. The *Buffalo Skull Dream Weaver Circle* is an excellent pattern to practice and experiment with the four ingredients.

1 The outer ring was created by using tightly packed, straight, diagonal lines; a medium-high temperature; and a slow rate of movement. Several layers of this stroke were burned until the area had a dark, even coloring.

2 The next ring is made of short, straight-line fill strokes (see Square 66 on page 57) on a medium temperature and with a medium time for burning, while the inner sections of the pie-shaped wedges are straight lines. The inner pie wedges were first darkly burned with widely spaced, straight, diagonal lines (see square 15 on page 57). Then, layers of random curls (see squares 33–37 on page 57) were applied over the lines. Once a medium-dark tone was achieved, one more layering of random curls was added along the inner edge of the circle to deepen this line.

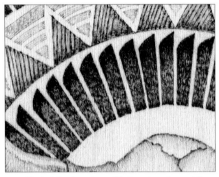

3 The last ring is made up of feather-shaped curved-line strokes (see squares 69–70 on page 57). These were burned at a high temperature setting and with a small dash-stroke pattern (see squares 1–5 on page 57) by letting the tool tip rest for a moment to create the dark tone. Along the outer edge of this feather shape, a second layer of dash-stroke pattern was added to darken the tips to a black coloring.

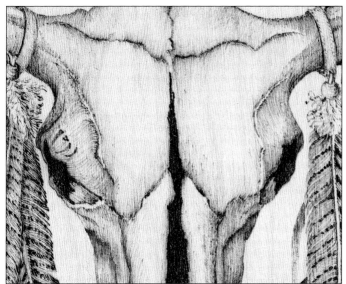

4 **The buffalo skull** design was burned using a fine-line texturing at low temperatures. This work is very similar to the work in *Our Daily Bread*. Layer upon layer of fine lines were added to darken the shadows of each area, giving the skull a three-dimensional finish. The black areas within the skull are filled with the small-dot pattern at a high temperature until these areas are as black as the inner circle feather shapes.

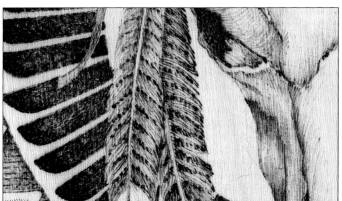

5 **The feathers** that hang from the buffalo's horns are done in short curved-line strokes (see square 70 on page 57). A central line to the feathers was first burned, and then finer lines were added, working from that centerline out toward the edge of the feather.

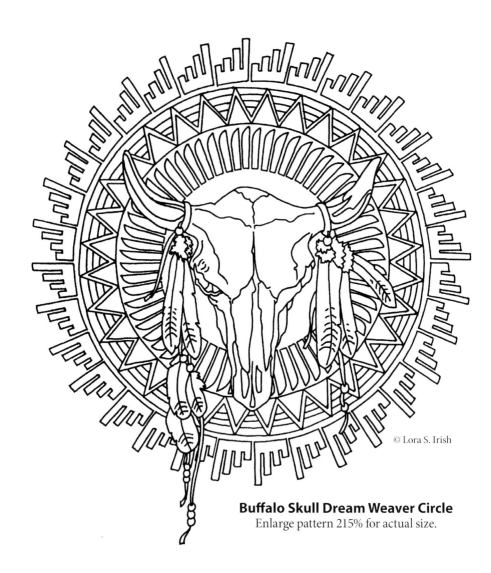

© Lora S. Irish

Buffalo Skull Dream Weaver Circle
Enlarge pattern 215% for actual size.

Texture Exercise:
Putting Textures Together

The *Solar Flare Sun Face* (pattern on page 93) is a fun pattern to try if you want to explore the multiple textures that you can use in woodburning (see the photo above). To add to the fun look of *Solar Flare Sun Face*, I chose a very grain-sculptured piece of heartwood birch plywood for the project. Not only is the sun face full of changing patterns and textures, but so is the unburned background of the wood because

of its dramatic graining. Try this design using the texture patterns that most interest you from the practice board—as well as experimental texture patterns of your own! Here again, we will be working with the whole pattern instead of using a portion of the pattern as we did with the previous exercises. I used a medium heat setting throughout this exercise.

This design, *Solar Flare Sun Face*, uses eight distinct textures: cross-hatching, dash strokes, wavy lines, random curls, seashell circles, herringbone, diagonal lines, and detail outlining. This was all worked on heartwood birch plywood, which adds more texture to the finished design because of the changing grain pattern in the wood.

1 **For my sample, I used tight-spaced cross-hatching** (see squares 24–32 on page 57) to establish the shadows and shading in the face. Adding more layers of cross-hatching created the darker facial shadings.

2 **Touching the tool tip to the wood** to burn tightly packed, small dots (see square 56 on page 57) gave the eyes, nostrils, and mouth the black-chocolate coloring.

3 **The wavy-line texture** (see square 42 on page 57) was used to create the sun face's mustache. Over this texturing, a light layering of random curls (see squares 33–37 on page 57) made the mustache darker where it touched the bottom of the nose.

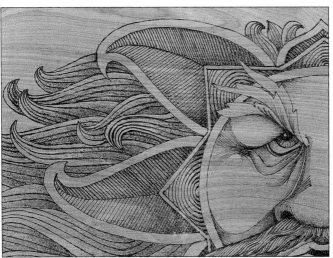

4 **The diamond shapes** that surround the sun face were filled with the seashell circle texture (see square 43 on page 57).

5 **The sun flare leaves** have a herringbone straight-line burn (see square 53 on page 57), worked from the centerline out toward the flare's edge. Detail lines were first burned into the curling flares that make up the hair. Over this detailing, random curls (see squares 33–37 on page 57) were laid to create the shading. New layers of random curls were burned to darken these flares where one flare tucked under another. The stars were filled in with two layers of diagonal lines.

6 **Once all of the texturing and shading were completed**, I added the outline burn to each element.

Solar Flare Sun Face
Enlarge pattern 268% for actual size.

© Lora S. Irish

Finding Tonal Values:

Composition of a Good Woodburning

Now that we have taken a look at how to create the various tones and textures with your woodburning tool, we want to take a look at how all of the elements interact to create a complete picture. Understanding tonal values, or the different shades of color that we've been discussing, is one of the keys to creating a pleasing finished project. These values can be used to give one element or area of a woodburning more emphasis than the rest of the design. They can also help you translate real images into a woodburning project.

In addition to tonal values, we'll explore a variety of techniques, including how to make the most of your unburned areas, effective ways to outline your projects, and how to use textures in conjunction with each other. By taking the time to learn both the techniques for creating shades and textures and the concepts for putting them all together, you'll be able to confidently woodburn a cohesive finished piece.

Understanding Tonal Values

If you have been working through the book from the beginning, you are already a little familiar with the concept of tonal values. Any time we have been working with shades of color, we have been working with tonal values. Understanding tonal value, also called gray scale, and its use in a woodburning pattern will greatly enhance the quality of your work.

What Exactly Are Tonal Values?

The human eye gathers information about an object or a scene in two separate ways: the amount of light that strikes an object and the color of the object. Once the eye has determined both the light value and color value of an object, the information is merged to create the image that we see. So, although we see a shiny red apple that casts a shadow, the eye first sees the shine and the shadow, then sees the red, and finally creates the total image of a three-dimensional, highlighted red object with a shadow.

Highlights and shadows are called tonal values and range from the darkest black to the brightest white area of an image. Shades of brown and gray are also considered tonal values. Colors, called hues, include the primary hues of red, yellow, and blue. You can mix hues and tonal values. As an example, pastel yellow is a mixture of the primary hue of yellow and the white tonal value. Navy blue is a mixture of the primary color blue and the tonal value of black.

Pyrography works in the same manner. First, we create the woodburning using tonal values from very dark brown through the palest tones of our wood surface. Once the burning is completed, coloring can be placed over top of the burned surface. This merges the two areas of information exactly as the human eye does.

Finding the Tonal Values in a Photo or Drawing

Whether you are working from a pencil drawing, a black-and-white photograph, or a burned sample from this book to create your woodburning, you will first want to number the tonal values from the darkest area of the image to the brightest white area. Exploring the finished burning of *The Philadelphia Derringer,* you will note that the woodburning is created in only one color. Every part of the design is brown. This is called a monochromatic image, mono meaning "one" and chromatic meaning "color." So, it is a one-color design. What creates the picture is the brown used in various tonal values. The work has areas that range from no burning at all to very pale browns to a black-brown value.

By numbering the values first, you can discover where your blackest and whitest points in the burning will be, discover areas of similar

value for easy burning, and identify each area before you begin. Throughout this section, I'll show you how to identify and number each of the different values in a photo.

As you are doing the value numbering of a photo or drawing, you will want to watch for areas that might cause you problems during the composition stage or woodburning process. This particular still life is set up in a triangular composition with the elements—the derringer, the books, and the pipes—all contained within the left and bottom section of the photo. The upper section and right side contain no elements. So, the bottom left of the photo is full, but the upper right half is empty. I wanted to work *The Philadelphia Derringer* on a rectangular board, so I added an old map, pinned to the wall, as a background element. This fills the empty area behind the still life. Since this map design was added after the photo and after the value numbering process, it is not shown in the photos. However, because the map will hang on the wall behind the still life, I worked the map in the same tonal value as the wall in the photo.

Value #1—Black (darkest value)

To establish the tonal values of a woodburned picture, begin with either a pencil drawing of your design or a photograph. If you have access to a computer and scanner, scan the photo into the computer. Using a graphics program, change that photo to gray scale. This removes all of the color information from the photo, leaving only the shadows and highlights. Most digital cameras on the market today have editing programs that can be used to make gray scale

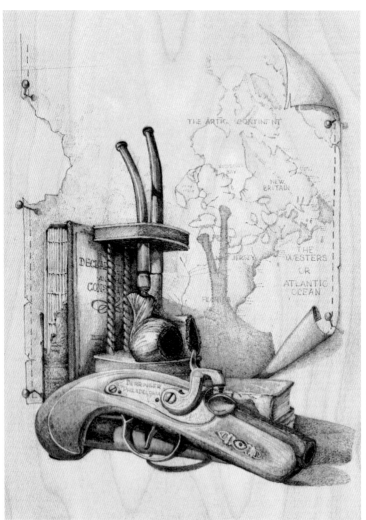

The Philadelphia Derringer is a good example of a tonal value woodburning. Note that the darkest areas of the burning are found in the shadows under the derringer, inside the briar pipes, and under the roof of the pipe rack. The palest, or lightest, values are used for the book pages, background map, and gunmetal.

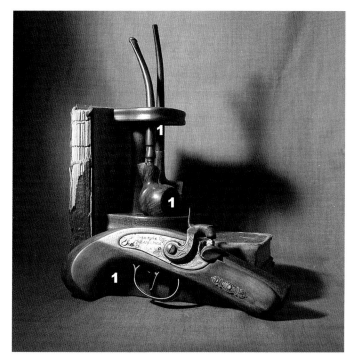

Figure A: The darkest areas of the photo are numbered. These shadows form the black, or darkest, value: Value #1.

images. Two of the many excellent graphics programs available to an artist are PaintShop® Pro and Adobe® Photoshop®. Please refer to the Help section of your computer program for use and instructions. I find it easiest to establish the tonal values of a still life by working from the darkest to the lightest areas. First, find the very black shadows of the photo and mark these as Value #1.

For the photo of the Derringer still life, the darkest areas (see Figure A) are the inside of the front briar pipe, the shadow cast by the derringer onto the books, and the area underneath the top section of the pipe rack. The smaller areas of black have not been numbered. They are the right edge of the standing book's binding, the area where the standing book's side meets the backdrop, the inside of the gun's barrel, and the shadow on the back pipe's stem.

Figure B: Value #2 comprises areas that are just a bit lighter than the black values of Value #1.

Value #2—Dark chocolate (dark value)

Next, look for black tones that are not quite as dark as those already noted. These are Value #2.

The photo shows Value #2 (see Figure B) on the lower portion of the right side of the standing book and in the large shadow on the backdrop. The left side of the backdrop in the photo would also be a Value #2; however, since our still life design will have an antique map as its background, this area in the photo will not become part of the finished burning. The added map will use the Value #2 setting of the backdrop.

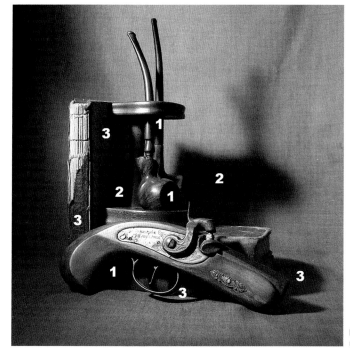

Value #3—Milk chocolate (medium-dark value)

Still working with the dark values of the photo, these areas that are just a touch paler than the last are marked as Value #3 (see Figure C). Notice that with each numbering you are looking for areas that are slightly lighter in value than the last.

The Value #3 areas are the upper portion of the standing book's right side, the front binding of the standing book, and the shadows under the trigger guard and to the right of the book stack.

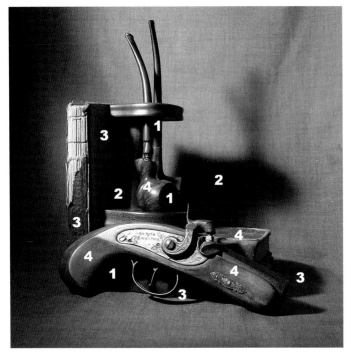

Figure D: Label the milky mocha colors as the medium values for Value #4.

Value #4—Coffee with cream (medium value)

You know that soft, milky mocha look that coffee with cream has? That's the tonal value that you now want to mark (see Figure D). It is the middle tonal value in this photo, or Value #4.

The middle values are located on the gunstock and the top cover of the book stack. The edges of the stacked books and the gun's hammer mechanism are also Value #4 but are too small to mark in the photo.

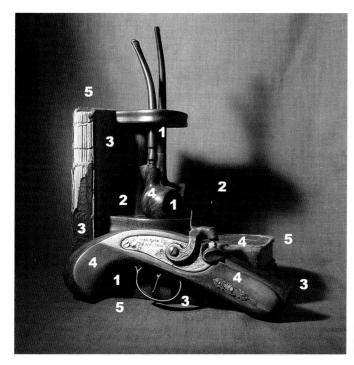

Figure E: Tanned leather colors make up the light-medium values of Value #5.

Value #5—Tanned leather (light-medium value)

Those areas that are lighter than the medium tones are next numbered as Value #5 (see Figure E).

Value #5 tones are the backdrop cloth sections to the right side of the book stack, below the derringer, and above the standing book. An antique map will appear in the pattern in these areas.

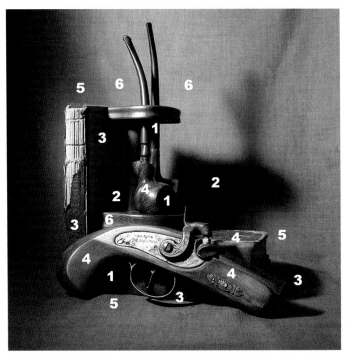

Figure F: Light values in the photo, colored like caramel candy, are marked as Value #6.

Value #6—Caramel (light value)

The pale tones of a woodburning often take on the coloring of a caramel candy and are noted as Value #6 (see Figure F).

For our sample, these pale shadings are found to the left and right of the pipe stems and in the base of the pipe rack. The two marked areas surrounding the pipe stems will be burned into the antique map background of the pattern.

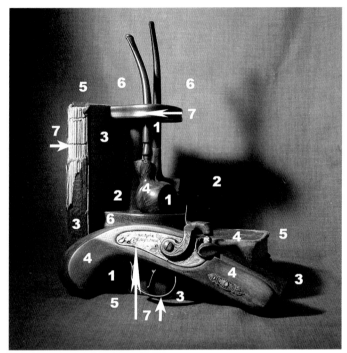

Figure G: The lightest values of the work, similar to a pale linen color, are noted as Value #7.

Value #7—Linen (palest value)

The palest values in a woodburning still have color in them. They are likened to a pale linen and become Value #7 (see Figure G).

The lightest shades of tonal value in this photo are found in the damaged area of the standing book's binding and as highlights in the pipe rack. The tipper guard edge and metal plate on the side of the derringer are also extremely pale. These areas are numbered as Value #7.

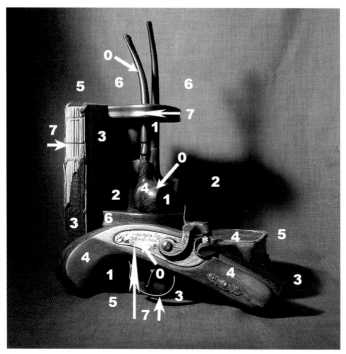

Figure H: The unburned portions of the design are Value #0.

Value #0—Unburned areas

There will be areas of any pattern that you do not woodburn. The original coloring of the wood, therefore, becomes the whitest areas of the work. These areas can be noted as Value #0, the zero representing the lack of burning. If I had not included the map in the final burning, all of the area in the background of the still life, except the cast shadows, would have been marked as Value #0 (see Figure H).

In this design, the metal plate beneath the pistol's hammer, the highlights on the briar pipe, and the highlight along the pipe stem have all been left unburned wood, so they are Value #0 areas.

Transferring the Values

Once the tonal values have been established, you can transfer those value numbers to a pattern for quick reference as you work (see Figure I). As a general rule of thumb, the larger the number of values that can be established in a design, the more realistic the finished burning will be. Photo-realistic woodburnings often begin with seven to nine distinct tonal values (see Figure J). More simplistic burnings may have three to five tonal values.

As a beginning woodburner, keep the number of tonal values to a minimum, between three and five. This keeps the number of different tonal values small as you learn to burn light, medium, and dark areas into your work. As you grow in this craft, you will discover that you are adding more and more levels of tonal value.

In the top row of squares in Figure J (see page 106), I have cut samples of each of the tonal values used in this burning and placed them in order from darkest to lightest so that you can see the progression of the tones. This row begins with a solid square of black color and ends with a solid square of beige that matches the birch wood that you can use as comparison to the burned values. The bottom row of squares is created to show some of the detailing and texturing used in *The Philadelphia Derringer*.

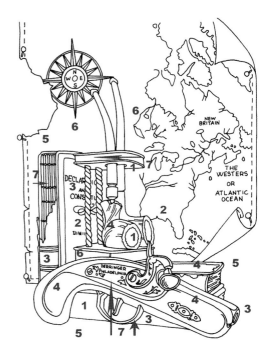

Figure I: By marking the value numbers on the traced pattern, you can create a map for the placement of your pale, medium, and dark tonal values.

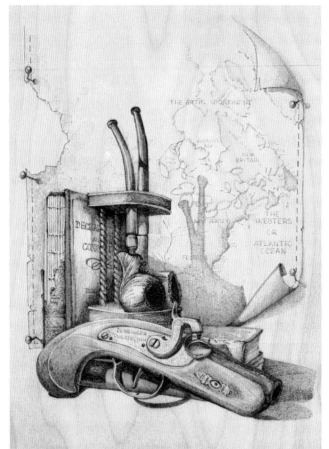

Figure J: You can see the value scale below the derringer burning that shows the wide variety of sepia tones you can achieve in woodburning. A black square has been added to provide a comparison to the very darkest tones; the unburned square of birch is equal to the whitest value. Below the tonal values you can see some of the different textures and strokes used in this burning to create those tonal values.

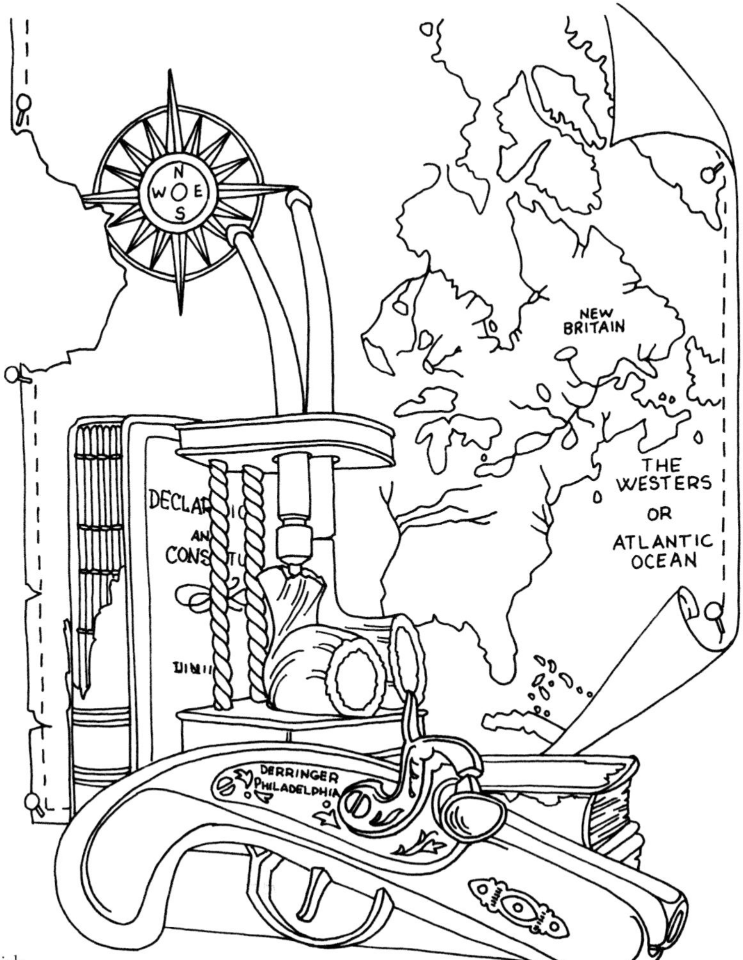
N
W
E
S
NEW BRITAIN
THE WESTERS OR ATLANTIC OCEAN
DERRINGER PHILADELPHIA

The Philadelphia Derringer

Enlarge pattern 183% for actual size.

Tonal Value Excercise:
The Pocket Watch

The Pocket Watch is perfect for learning more about tonal values. This design has been broken down into six steps: one for the outlining of the design; four steps focusing on one tonal value each; and one step for finishing.

The Pocket Watch measures 8" wide by 12" high (20.5 x 30.5cm). My sample was worked on birch plywood using a variable-temperature tool and a writing tip, but you can use a one-temperature tool also. The thermostat temperatures were changed throughout this burning. The textures used in this project are shown on the practice board (see the following squares on page 57: wide crosshatch 15–23; tight crosshatch 24–32; tightly packed spots 56; scrubbie lines 61–64; and curved lines 69–70). Throughout this step-by-step project, I will be showing the settings that work for me with my variable-temperature tool. You will want to adjust those settings to fit your practice settings chart according to the wood that you have chosen to burn.

This will be a very quick project because the face of the clock, the largest pattern section, is not burned. It remains the original color of the wood. As you work, focus on establishing four individual color tones and keeping those color tones the same throughout the design.

Although the finished piece was worked as a picture, this would be a delightful design made as an actual wall clock (see Creating a Real Wall Clock on page 114).

1 **Begin the work by lightly sanding** your plywood with fine-grit sandpaper. Remove any sanding dust with a lint-free cloth or large drafter's dusting brush. Make a tracing of the pattern onto vellum or onionskin tracing paper. Rub the back of the tracing paper with a soft pencil until you have created a dark, even layer of graphite. Tape the pattern paper to your board and retrace the pattern lines. Trace only those lines that you need to guide you through the work. With a white artist's eraser, rub off any smudges or streaks left during the tracing process. Set your thermostat to a medium-high temperature. With the writing tip, outline all of the pattern lines.

The Pocket Watch design uses several important texturing patterns from page 57: the scrubbie-line stroke (squares 61–64); tightly packed spots (square 56); and the curved-line stroke (squares 69–70). The cross-hatching pattern, whether worked with wide spacing (squares 15–23) or tight spacing (squares 24–32), is used in this design for the medium and pale shaded areas of the pocket watch's body.

Tracing. The pattern for *The Pocket Watch* contains lines for the element outlines as well as guidelines for the five different tonal value areas. These tonal value guidelines are most apparent in the outer ring of the watch. In my sample, I have traced only the element outlines of the pattern. You can also trace the tonal value guidelines if you wish.

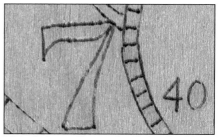

Outlining. Burning your outline on a medium setting keeps the outlining from becoming too dark early in the work. You can reburn sections of the outlines later to darken them as necessary.

2 **The burning for this pattern** has been broken down into four tonal values: very dark; dark; medium; and light. Set your thermostat to a medium-high temperature. Use a slow, scrubbie-line stroke (squares 61–64 on page 57) to fill in the very dark tonal values on your clock. For some of the small areas, you can fill that section by touching the tip of the tool to the wood and then lifting the tip. This burns small tightly packed black spots (square 56 on page 57). When using the texture of small dark spots, the closer you pack the spots into the area, the darker that area will become.

Very dark tones. The darkest areas of the watch pattern are the numbers, the triangles on the circular minute dial, the outer ring of the dial, and the inner circle on the seconds dial. There are several areas of very dark shadow in the winding set area, along the left side of the watch body, the watch hands, and in the upper section of the twisted cord. Mark the registration lines on the sides of the cylinder.

Very dark tones (Value #1) map

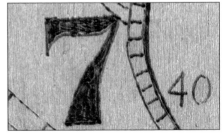

Very dark tones, close up. The numbers are the most important elements of this design. By burning them to the darkest tonal value, you give them both strength and visual emphasis.

3 **Reduce the temperature slightly** and begin working the dark areas. I have used both the scrubbie-line fill and a short-curved line fill (squares 69–70 on page 57) for my texturing. The burning lines in both of these textures are tightly packed to create the color tone.

Dark tones (Value #2) map

Dark tones. This burning of the dark tones includes the remaining portions of the clock hands, a large portion of the left side of the winding stem area and areas in the twisted cord, both above and below the clock, and the tassel. A ring of dark-tone shadow goes around the clock body. One small section on the lower left side of the clock body remains unburned.

Dark tones, close up. Notice that with a variable-temperature tool you can completely fill an area, allowing little or no unburned wood to show, using medium-toned coloring. If you are using a one-temperature tool, you may wish to use a wide crosshatch texture (squares 15–23 on page 57) in this area, letting some of the wood color show to achieve an overall dark but not black tone.

4 **For the medium-toned values**, I have left the temperature setting the same. Use a tight crosshatch pattern (squares 24–32 on page 57) that allows some of the original wood coloring to show through the burning to fill in the medium areas.

Medium tones. An inner circle of shading in the clock body, especially in the upper left side, is worked using a medium tone. There are also medium-toned areas in the winding stem area, the twisted cord, and the tassel. Notice that there is a section in the clock body's left side adjacent to the clock dial that remains unburned.

Medium tones (Value #3) map

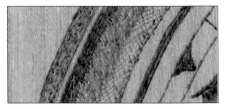

Medium tones, close up. The temperature setting has not been changed between the dark-tone step and the medium-tone step. The color changes instead because of the texturing pattern. Crosshatch texturing allows some of the original wood to show through the burned lines, therefore giving a lighter or paler look than tightly packed lines burned at the same temperature. If you are using a one-temperature tool and you crosshatched the dark tones, allow more original wood between your crosshatch burned lines for this step.

5 The temperature setting has been reduced to medium-low. Using a scrubbie-line stroke, burn in the light areas. When you have completed the burning, you should have four very distinct color tones in the work, with the face of the clock remaining the original color of the wood.

Light tones. A light value is used to fill in the minute ring of the clock dial and the seconds dial, the inner ring on the clock dial, and much of the right side of the clock body. The lower side of the open loop in the winding stem is completed in light value, as are the forward sections of the twisted cord.

Light tones (Value #4) map

Light tones, close-up. When this step is complete, you should have four distinct tonal values ranging from very dark to light. The background to the clock dial remains unburned. If you are using a one-temperature tool, unplug your tool. Allow it to cool down, and then plug it in again. At that point, burn the light tones before your tool reaches its maximum heat setting.

6 **Once the burning is complete**, lightly sand the surface of the project with fine-grit sandpaper or a foam-core emery board to remove the roughness. Next, use a white artist's eraser over the burning to remove any pencil lines from the original tracing. Set your work where you can look over the project. Check that you have both very dark chocolate areas in the work as well as very pale linen colors to create contrast in the work. Are there middle tones of medium brown and coffee-with-cream shades?

Even though you have worked through the steps of the project, new layering or shading can be added at this point to strengthen your design. This is an excellent time to sign and date your work in the lower right-hand corner. Once any touchups are finished, re-sand lightly, dust, and seal your project with either polyurethane or a paste wax.

Creating a Real Wall Clock

Once you've mastered the tonal values, you may want to create this project as the background of an actual wall clock. Your woodburning becomes the clock face with battery clock hands to keep time.

- **Step 1:** Purchase battery clockworks. Battery clocks come with different lengths of shafts that go through the wood and hold the clock hands. Be sure to match the length of this shaft to the thickness of your wood.

- **Step 2:** Measure the length of the big hand of the battery clock. Then, reduce the size of the burning pattern so that the length of the big hand in the pattern is identical to the length of the battery clock's big hand. This will be an approximate pattern width of 5½" to 6" (14 to 15.25cm).

- **Step 3:** Trace this small-sized pattern to the plywood, but leave out the hands of the pattern clock. Mark a ¼" (6.35mm) margin beyond the outline of the clock.

- **Step 4:** With a scroll saw, cut out the clock along the ¼" (6.35mm) margin line. Drill a hole in the center of the clock that matches the diameter of the battery clock's shaft.

- **Step 5:** Burn the pattern. You might consider adding a manufacturer's name in the clock face area directly under the number 12. Use your surname as the manufacturer (examples: Johnson's Clockworks or Smith's Swiss Movements).

- **Step 6:** Once the burning is complete, mount the battery clock through the hole you drilled.

The Pocket Watch
Enlarge pattern 225%
for actual size.

© Lora S. Irish

PROJECT

Little Book of Pyrography

Step-by-Step:
The Dragonette

The *Dragonette* is a wonderful beginner's project that will allow you to experiment with your different tip styles and with the tonal values you can create with your woodburner. Because the dragonette is a mythical creature, this pattern is very adaptable. So, if one area becomes a little lighter or a little darker or if your outlines do not exactly follow the tracing lines, this design will still finish beautifully.

The dragonette has claimed a battle shield as his favorite resting spot. With wings flared, he is quite ready to protect his territory. In fact, he is so intense in his attitudes that he has twisted his tail into a Celtic knot. With bold, dark tonal areas contrasting against the original color of the wood in the shield's cross, this pattern makes an excellent beginner's project.

The original design was worked on a 9" by 9" (22.75 x 22.75cm) basswood pre-routed wall plaque. The design itself measures 7" by 7" (17.75 x 17.75cm). It was burned using a variable-temperature tool and a writing tip; however, this project is very suitable for a one-temperature tool.

Tonal values for *Dragonette*

Little Book of Pyrography

Steps 1-6: Transferring the pattern

Trace the pattern onto the wood using vellum or onionskin tracing paper and graphite pencils.

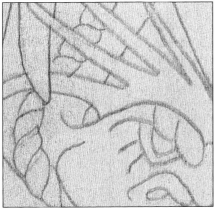

Clean up smudges with a white artist's eraser.

1 Begin the work by lightly sanding the wood with fine-grit sandpaper.

2 Remove any sanding dust with a lint-free cloth or a drafter's dusting brush.

3 Make a copy of the pattern from this book on vellum or onionskin tracing paper.

4 Rub the back of the tracing paper with a soft #4B to #6B pencil until you have created a dark, even layer of graphite.

5 Tape the paper to your board, graphite side down, and retrace the pattern lines. Trace only those lines that you need to guide you through the work.

6 With a white artist's eraser, rub off any smudges or streaks left during the tracing process.

Steps 7-10: Shading one side of the body

Here, one side of the dragonette's body is shaded with short curved lines.

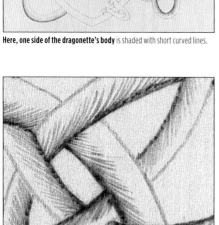

Be sure to shade the correct side of the tail as it twists and turns.

7 Begin the project by shading the top portion of the dragonette's body where it disappears under the front wing. Use a medium temperature setting and a short curved-line stroke (see square 70 on page 57).

8 As the body flows down the plaque, the shaded side will become the bottom portion of the body where the tail twists under the shield. Limit the shading to the bottom side of the tail where it reappears on the right side of the shield.

9 Follow this side as the tail travels through the knot, whether that side is on the top or bottom of the dragonette's body. Stop the shading where the tail feathers begin.

10 When the short curved-line shading is complete, add an outline along that side of the dragon's body and tail.

Steps 11-12: Shading the remaining body

Now, shade the other side of the dragonette's body.

11 Repeat the shading steps for the remaining side of the dragonette's body. Notice how the short curved-line stroke for this side follows the direction established when you worked the first side. The curved lines from the two sides work toward each other, creating a broken S-shaped line.

12 When the shading is complete, add an outline to the second side of the body.

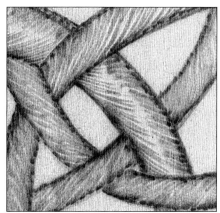

It is much easier to shade this half of the dragonette's body now that the other side is done.

Steps 13-15: Belly-fold shading

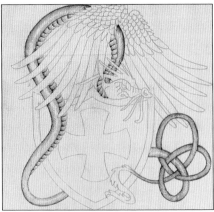

13 As with the body, the belly folds will be worked in two phases, one side at a time.

14 Begin your work where the neck joins the head. Shade on the lower outside edge of the belly fold. This shading is created with short, curved lines that radiate from the lower, outer point.

15 As you work through the belly folds, limit the shading to the lower portion for each new fold.

The belly-fold shading has been completed.

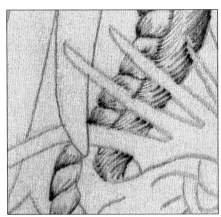

Use a short, curved line that radiates from the lower outer point of the belly fold.

Steps 16-18: Belly shading for the remaining side

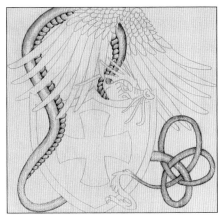

16 The second stage of the belly shading is worked where the belly fold meets the body. Use a medium-high heat setting.

17 In this angled area, burn a small, very dark, triangle shape. This separates the top section of one belly fold from the bottom section of the next belly fold. Because this triangle is worked to a darker tone, it pushes the belly fold deeply into its junction with the body.

18 Add a dark, comma-shaped line along the outside edge of each belly fold. Do not completely outline these folds; you are just accenting them.

Burn a dark triangle wherever the belly fold meets the body.

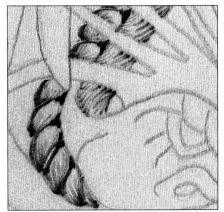

Burn the dark triangles using a medium-high setting to emphasize the separation of the belly folds.

Steps 19-20: Adding wing shadows to the body

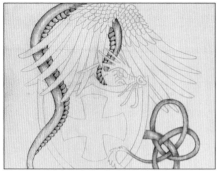

The **random curl stroke** creates the wings' shadows to the body.

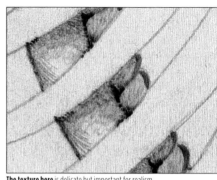

The **texture here** is delicate but important for realism.

19 On a medium temperature setting and using a random curl stroke (see squares 33–37 on page 57), add a light layering of shadow to the body beneath each wing feather. This light shadowing implies that the wing lies over the body and therefore casts a shadow on that part of the body.

20 Shadowed areas appear on the body on both sides of the wing's shoulder and beneath the five long wing feathers using the random curl stroke.

Steps 21-33: Detailing the face

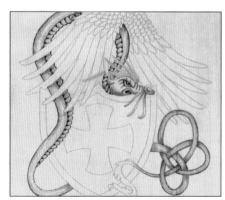

Now, shade the other side of the dragonette's body.

21 The shading in the face is done with short curved lines. Set the tool to a medium temperature. Then, shade the nose ridges working from the left top.

22 Shade the upper eye ridges and the nostril area starting at the bottom left.

23 Burn the folds to the left of the eye with the short lines close to the eye.

24 Start curved lines at the mouth area where the chin and jaw rest on the shield and pull them upward, arching to the left.

Little Book of Pyrography

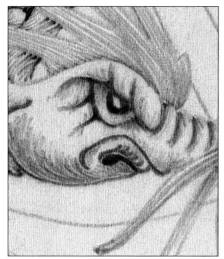

It is much easier to shade this half of the dragonette's body now that the other side is done.

25 Fill the nose tendrils with light-toned, long curved lines that follow the direction of that tendril.

26 Work the crest with long curved lines that start at the skull and flow to the points of the crest.

27 When the shading is complete, turn the temperature up slightly. Add a separating line between each nose ridge.

28 Outline the bottom edge of the upper eye ridges.

29 Use a large comma stroke to create the nostril.

30 Detail along the lip line of the mouth and along the jaw line.

31 Increase the temperature; then, add the mouth with a short scrubbie-line stroke.

32 Texture the eye with the same stroke, leaving a small white area for the eye's highlight.

33 The folds to the left of the eye are darkly detailed, and a small spot of darkness is added to the inside corner of the eye.

Steps 34-35: Long wing feathers

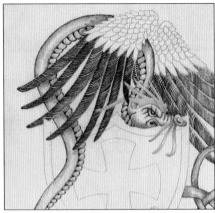

34 For the feathering of the wings, turn your tool to a hot temperature. Working the long front-wing feather, use a curved-line stroke that starts on the outside edge of the feather and flows upward toward the inside edge. A dark starting point will appear naturally along this outer edge.

35 The long back-wing feathers are worked in the same manner, but turn the tool temperature down to a medium setting.

The front-wing feathers are much darker than the back-wing feathers.

Start the stroke from the edge of the feather and curve inward.

Step 36: Adding a second layer to the back

36 After the long back-wing feathers are completed, add a second layer in the area of the wing directly behind the dragonette's face and neck. Lay the tool tip back into the already-burned curved line and re-burn that line. This will lightly darken this area of the wing to create more contrast between the wing and the face.

Re-burning the feathers surrounding the dragonette's neck and face will emphasize the border there.

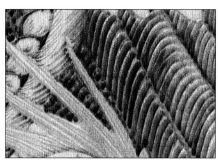

Burning a second layer will subtly darken the area.

Step 37: Outlining the shoulder feathers

37 Setting the tool tip to a high temperature, outline each of the shoulder feathers.

Outline the shoulder feathers.

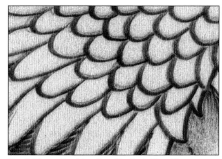

Use a high temperature to burn the outline; the dark line will be needed later.

Steps 38-41: Burning the shoulder feathers and tail

Use the short scrubbie-line stroke to shade each individual shoulder feather.

38 Keep the tool on a high setting and use a short scrubbie-line stroke (see squares 61–64 on page 57) to shade the top section of each shoulder feather. Because the scrubbie-line stroke is applied at a slightly faster pace, this shadowing will become slightly paler than the slowly burned outline of the previous step.

39 Outline each individual feather in the shoulder area using high heat and a long fish-scale texture (see square 57 on page 57).

40 Turn the tool temperature down slightly to a medium-high setting. Working from the right side of the tail tip, pull long, curved lines through the tail tip toward the left side.

41 Outline both sides of the tail tip.

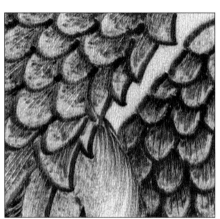

The dark outline from the previous section guides the placement of the scrubbie-line shading.

Steps 42-43: Shading the body of the shield

42 The mid-ground area of the shield will be worked in two stages. On a medium-high setting, first outline the center cross design in the shield.

43 A random curl stroke (see squares 33–37 on page 57) is used next to fill in the area of the shield between the central cross design and the outer border of the shield. This random curl stroke will have lots of variations in color tones, giving this area of the shield extra interest.

Outline the cross and use the random curl stroke to fill the inner shield.

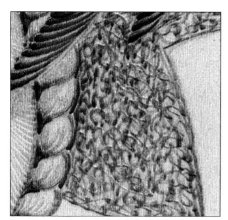

The random curl stroke adds a lot of variation in color tones.

Steps 44-46: Adding extra layering to the shield

44 Notice in the photo that the area along the top section and the right side of the shield is darker than the rest of this area. These darker sections require a second layering of the random curl stroke.

45 In both the left and right corners of this mid-ground, add a third layer of work. These added layers give the shield its bowed effect.

46 Turn the tool setting to high and, using a dash stroke (see squares 1–5 on page 57), fill in the outer border with a very dark color tone. Work this outer border with very tightly packed strokes until it has a solid black or dark chocolate coloring.

The outer border of the shield has been filled with a dash stroke, and another layer of texture has been burned onto the outer parts of the inner shield.

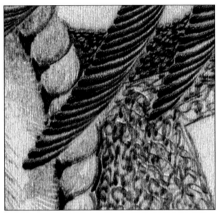

The dark value of the dash stroke adds contrast between the beige of the cross and the shifting value of the shield.

Steps 47-52: Finishing

Sealing your *Dragonette* piece with polyurethane or a paste wax will protect it from the dust, dirt, and oil that may collect over the years.

47 When the burning is complete, lightly sand the surface of the project with fine-grit sandpaper or a foam-core emery board to remove the roughness.

48 Next, rub a white artist's eraser over the burning to remove any pencil lines from the original tracing.

49 Remove any dust or eraser particles with a lint-free cloth or a drafter's dusting brush.

50 Set your work where you can look over the project. Check that you have very dark chocolate areas as well as very pale linen colors to create contrast in the work. Are there middle tones of medium brown and coffee-with-cream shades? Even though you have worked through the steps of this project, new layering or shading can be added at this point to strengthen your design.

51 This is an excellent time to sign and date your work in the lower right-hand corner.

52 Once any touch-ups are finished, re-sand lightly, dust with a lint-free cloth, and seal your project with either polyurethane or a paste wax.

The finished *Dragonette*

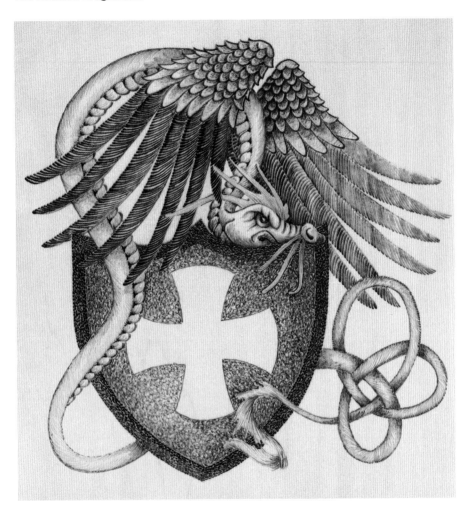

Little Book of Pyrography

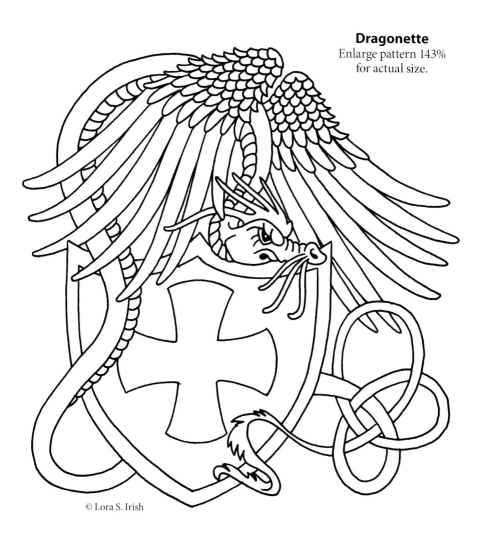

Dragonette
Enlarge pattern 143%
for actual size.

© Lora S. Irish

Dragonette Chessboard

Here is the same *Dragonette* design that you just worked but patterned for a game board or chessboard. The Celtic knot tail design has been increased to include a Celtic knot between the opposing dragonettes. Because this piece was worked on birch plywood—a harder wood than basswood—the tonal values are lighter than the deep color tones created on the *Dragonette* plaque. The width of each burned line tends to be slightly thinner on a harder wood than the width of a line done on a softer wood.

This *Dragonette Chessboard* was worked using the same step-by-step process as the *Dragonette* (with the shield; see page 117). When the dragonettes were completed, the dark borderline surrounding the chessboard was burned in the same fashion as the dark borderline of the *Dragonette* (with the shield). The dark squares on the chessboard were burned on a medium setting using tight-spaced crosshatch (see squares 24–32 on page 57).

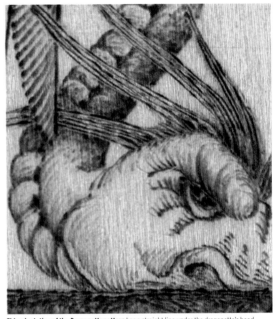

This adaptation of the *Dragonette* pattern has a straight line under the dragonette's head.

The *Dragonette Chessboard* features tight-spaced crosshatch on the dark squares.

Dragonette Chessboard with Coloring

When the burning for this chessboard was completed and the work sanded, I used watercolors to add bright colors (see larger photo and pattern on pages 139–140). The watercolors were first placed on a glass tile or plate and then were thinned with water until they were fairly transparent. The paints were then applied using soft sable brushes by floating a light coat on each area. One color can be laid over another color to create shading or to deepen the original color. Be sure to allow the first layering of color to dry well before adding more. Any mistakes can easily be lifted with a wet brush.

1 Begin by applying one coat of the highlight color throughout the entire designated area. Do all of the highlight colors at one time. Allow the work to dry well, about one half hour.

2 Where one element of a design goes underneath a second element, the first element will have a shadow area. Add the shading color to these areas of the design. Allow the highlight colors to remain unworked in the areas of the element that are farther removed from an overlapping element.

3 In any small, tight areas where one element tucks under another, add one more layer of the dark shading color. For instance, for any one loop in the dragonette's body where both ends of that loop tuck under another element, you will have a small section of dark shading color, a wider section of shading color, a large area of highlight color, then back to the shading and dark shading colors.

4 Once all the coloring has been applied, allow the board to dry overnight. Then give the chessboard several light coats of spray polyurethane. Two holes can be drilled along the top edge of the plywood board to string a leather handle for hanging. Your chessboard can decorate your wall when it is not being used for your latest game of chess.

Make the chessboard
come alive
with watercolors.

Dragonette Chessboard Color Chart

Most areas of this design will use two different colors to create the final effect. The first color—the highlight color—is applied to establish the general color of the entire element's area. For example, the entire face and body of the dragonette is first painted with yellow ochre. Once this highlight color has dried, a second color, called the shading color, is applied to any area of the element that tucks under or touches an adjacent area. For example, the neck of the dragonette is shaded with verde green where the neck touches the base of the head. The neck is also shaded with verde green where it tucks under the wings.

Area	Highlight Color	Shading Color
Body and face	Yellow ochre	Verde green
Tail tip	Deep yellow	Yellow ochre
Long wing feathers	Verde green	Light turquoise
Celtic knot line	Yellow ochre	Burnt sienna
Shadowing for all areas	—	Raw umber
Dark squares	—	Raw umber
Light squares	—	50% yellow ochre and 50% burnt sienna (mixed half and half)

Dragonette Chessboard

Enlarge pattern 273% for actual size.

© Lora S. Irish

Gallery

With the right amount of dedication and practice, nearly anyone can learn pyrography. It's an exciting craft that can easily impress. Once you familiarize yourself with the pyrography tools and practice your technique, you will be ready to tackle more complex projects. Use the projects and patterns in this gallery as practice to continue your journey to the advanced levels of pyrography.

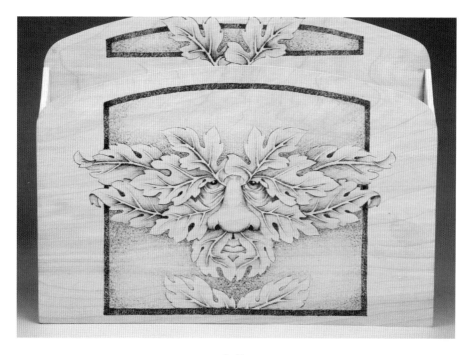

Goldfish
Enlarge pattern 159% for actual size.

Goldfish

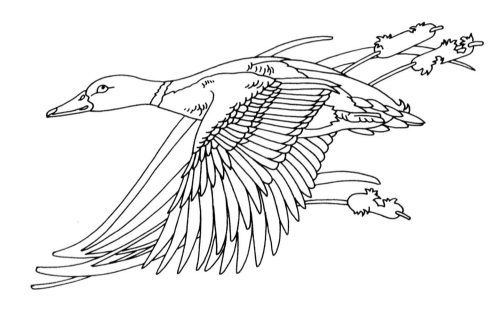

© Lora S. Irish

Mallard Drake
Enlarge pattern 200% for actual size.

Mallard Drake

© Lora S. Irish

Western Horse

Enlarge pattern 200% for actual size.

Western Horse

© Lora S. Irish

Oak Man
Enlarge pattern 258% for actual size.

Oak Man

© Lora S. Irish

The Country Church
Enlarge pattern 272% for actual size.

The Country Church

© Lora S. Irish

Grandpa's Pride and Joy
Enlarge pattern 200% for actual size.

Grandpa's Pride and Joy

© Lora S. Irish

Horned Owl
Enlarge pattern 285% for actual size.

Horned Owl

© Lora S. Irish

Harrisburg Star Barn
Enlarge pattern 200% for actual size.

Harrisburg Star Barn

Index

About the Author

Internationally known artist Lora S. Irish is the author of 28 woodcarving, pyrography, and craft pattern books, including *Great Book of Carving Patterns*, *World Wildlife Patterns for the Scroll Saw*, *The Art and Craft of Pyrography*, *Relief Carving the Wood Spirit*, *Great Book of Celtic Patterns*, and many more. Winner of the Woodcarver of the Year award, Lora is a frequent contributor to *Woodcarving Illustrated* and *Scroll Saw Woodworking & Crafts* magazines. Working from her rural mid-Maryland home studio, she is currently exploring new crafts and hobbies, including wire jewelry, metal sheet jewelry, piece patch and appliqué quilting, gourd carving, gourd pyrography, and leather crafts. Visit her at *www.LSIrish.com*.

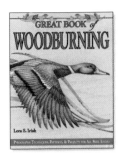
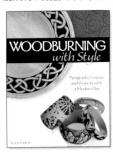
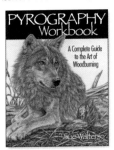
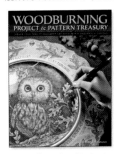